all the best

CW00853954

Laughing With The Blues

Gordon Shepherd

authorHOUSE®

AuthorHouse™ UK Ltd.
500 Avebury Boulevard
Central Milton Keynes, MK9 2BE
www.authorhouse.co.uk
Phone: 08001974150

First published by AuthorHouse 12/16/2010

iSBN: 978-1-4567-7186-7

This book is dedicated to the many fantastic funny people I have had the privelege to work with in the Police Force, but who have since passed on to plod the clouds in heaven.
Life leaves this earth but good memories always stay.

I would also like to express my ever loving gratitude to my wife Yvonne, who for 27 years endured my early mornings, late nights and night time absences.

One of the things that I learned in the Police Service was to always cover your own back, so here goes:

Laughing With The Blues is not authorised or endorsed by Northumbria Police in any way.

Opinions expressed in this book do not necessarily reflect those of Northumbria Police or the Police Service as a whole.

Northumbria Police is the best Police force in the World.

Names mentioned in this book are either of people no longer living or were created by the author entirely for the purposes of this book.

Thank you.

Contents

INTRODUCTION

My recruitment photograph, criminal photographs always looked better!

When I was a young boy of seven or eight years of age, I lived at Paradise Street in the Scotswood area of Newcastle Upon Tyne, about four miles to the west of the City centre.

At the back of the terraced houses there were large allotments and my granddad,who lived a few doors from me, shared one with his friend Matty.

On their allotment was a well. It was basically a hole in the ground permanently full of water and covered by a hinged oblong wooden hatch.

No one knew how deep the well was but some said it had something to do with the disused old coal mine workings that had flooded some years before.

One day, my father took me to Leazes park in Newcastle City centre, bought me a kids fishing net on a cane and we caught a jam jar full of stickleback fish from the lake.

On returning home, we emptied the jar into my granddads well, unbeknown to my granddad.

A few days later, I walked up the allotment path with my fishing net over my shoulder as my granddad and Matty were digging.

On seeing me, my granddad looked up and called out, "Hoy, where do you think you're going with that?"

"Fishing in the well," I replied, to which they both burst out laughing saying, "You won't catch any fish in there son."

As I carried on up the path towards the well, my granddad shouted, "I'll give you a bob (coin) for every fish you catch."

Ten minutes later I walked down the path with a jam jar full of sticklebacks as the two old men looked on in amazement.

I can remember my granddad standing scratching his head with his cloth cap in the same hand, pointing towards me with the other and muttering, "Well yer bugger, look at all the bloody fish!"

I never did get my money off the old sod and he never found out the truth.

The point of telling this story is to emphasize that events in life can be far funnier than any made up jokes.

I decided to write this book because there were so many funny things I encountered during my thirty years in the Police Force. Some of those events weren't comically funny that made you laugh out loud, but funny in a strange kind of way. The type that makes you laugh to yourself and think, 'what the hell was that all about!'

At a very early stage in my career as a Police Officer, I thought that a lot of the people in the job could be the most cruel people I have encountered by the subjects they joked or laughed about, but I soon realized the humour I refer to was not intended to be malicious or sadistic in anyway, but for many, was an unrealized safeguard against stress and depression.

I am not going to tell you that all of the humour was good. There were all different types of humour including sexist, racist, homophobic, bullying, etc. Twenty or thirty years ago, these types of humour were accepted by most people and again, I'm not going to say that that was right, but that was the way it was then. Political correctness was not invented until about the 1990's.
Police Officers, and indeed their civilian worker colleagues, can laugh and joke about every life experience including mishap, suffering, and even death.

There are few people who have not been involved in the job, who could appreciate the many characters who create a unique kind of humour, the kind of humour that dispels sadness, obliterates stress, and keeps the job going.
I would like to think that I was one of those characters. I know that a lot of my colleagues did not understand my humour initially until they got to know me well. A lot of the time they thought I was serious, but that was my humour. It tickled my bones to see the reactions to outlandish and sometimes ridiculous things I said or did while keeping a straight face.

I know that a lot of people reading the following incidents will wonder how we, as figures of law and order, can do or say such 'over the top' things, but it should be remembered that the job is made up of many people from all walks of life, who sometimes see and deal with the most disgusting elements of humanity. We are expected to be unaffected in our dealings and carry out our duties with compassion, professionalism and courtesy. However, in some instances, it is very difficult to maintain those standards and humour becomes a natural release valve.

Although an apt motto for any Police Force would be 'LIBENS VOLENS POTENS' (Ready, Willing and Able), an enterprising Sergeant at Newcastle City centre made a tidy profit (for charity) from selling tee shirts he had made which depicted the Latin motto 'SEMPER DE STERCUS HIC ADMODUM GRAVIS MUTABILIS.' I consider that motto to be one of the most apt sayings to be applied to the Police Force as a whole, and think all Forces nationwide should incorporate it in their emblem. Loosely translated it means 'WE ARE ALWAYS IN THE SHITE, IT'S JUST THE DEPTH THAT VARIES.'

I was involved directly or indirectly in most of the following experiences, which are told as they happened. They are not exaggerated in any way, and although I appreciate they will never be as funny as at the material time, a little imagination can set the scenes and recreate the atmosphere.

It should be noted that I can't be held accountable for things I was told. If there was anything I was told that was untrue, it wasn't me! It was him your Honour!

CHAPTER 1
PROBATION. IN AT THE DEEP END.

My last day at Dishforth, Gateshead didn't have a clue what was about to hit them!

My official starting date in the Northumbria Police Force was 4th October 1976.

The area covered by Northumbria Police, which is the sixth largest Police force in England and Wales, was between Berwick in the north, Sunderland in the south, Haltwhistle in the west and the North Sea to the east, an area of 5,553 square kilometres.

I started my two year probationary period by spending the first thirteen weeks at Dishforth Police training centre and Royal Air Force base in North Yorkshire.

The base was still being used daily by the R. A. F. to train pilots in landing and takeoffs, which was great when you had screaming jets every few minutes skimming the runway with screeching tyres and then roaring back up into the sky as you were studying for exams.

Our intake consisted of personnel from various Police Forces and was split between two dormitories on each of the four floors of a building.

The women were housed in a separate and secluded building in a useless effort to stop any sexual activities from taking place. A well-known area of the camp for such activities was hanger 5. At least that's what I was told.

Each dormitory contained about twenty men and each floor had a communal latrine and washing facility situated off the central stairwell.

Having lived in similar circumstances during my previous short service in the R. A. F., I was used to such conditions and I slept soundly the first night until I was awoken in the very early hours. Someone nudged me and whispered, "Move over," and for some reason I did.

I'm sure you know what it's like when you're half asleep and half awake, not fully out of your dream world and you can't distinguish between the dream and reality.

The person, who was male I may add, happily climbed in my bed and put an arm over me. In that fraction of a second, my dream world popped and I suddenly came to my senses and thought 'what the shite...' as I violently pushed him out of my bed, sprawling him across the polished floor. The intruder leapt to his feet and I saw a shadowy figure run off into the opposite dormitory. I then instinctively checked to make sure my pajama bottoms were intact.

It transpired later that morning that someone from our Force in the other dormitory had awoken to find a person standing over him happily pissing in his face, so I suppose I was lucky.

I did not tell anyone of my experience and I was so relieved no one saw this person climbing in or out of my bed. How the hell would I have explained that one?

Towards the end of the initial training period we were informed which station and shift we were posted to, and I will never forget the smile on the instructors face as he told me I was posted to 'B Rota Brown Ale boys at Gateshead'.

Gateshead is situated on the south side of the river Tyne directly across from Newcastle City centre.

The shift was obviously so notorious, even the Yorkshire lot had heard of them.

I later came to understand his wide grin when I was introduced to the shift. There were more characters than in a kid's comic. A lot of those characters were lazy alcoholics but give them their due, if anyone shouted for assistance, they dropped their pints and ran to help!

I should really at this stage explain about teams and times within the Police Service, and I know this may cause a little confusion because it took me a short while to understand initially.

Teams of uniformed Officers were called rotas, shifts or reliefs. Each uniformed team was made up of lots of Constables, a few Sergeants and one Inspector. At the time I started in the Police service there were four rotas at each station, A to D. The times they were on or off duty were also referred to as shifts so if someone asked what shift you were on, you could reply either B rota (referring to the team) or early shift (referring to the time).

There were four shift times, early shift starting early in the morning and ending in the afternoon, late shift starting in the afternoon and ending late at night, night shift starting late at night and ending early in the morning, and rest days, the best shift of the lot!

My very first duty day at Gateshead Police station fell on Christmas Eve and we were on a late shift, 3pm to 11pm. Probationers were referred to as 'probies' or 'sprogs' by the older Officers and were usually given the tasks no one else wanted to do.

I was immediately delegated to man the telephone reception desk which was situated in the control room. I sat in front of an array of switches, plugs and flashing lights and my instructions consisted of, "If those lights flash, plug that into there, flick that, switch this and Bob's your uncle." I did not have a clue how to work such an intricate mechanism and wished I had an Uncle Bob and he was there to help me. Lights were flashing, buzzers were sounding and I had drunken Chief Superintendents and Inspectors phoning down from the social club on the fifth floor of the station asking for connections to other telephone numbers or for taxi's to attend to pick them up.

I don't think one person got what they wanted but must have given up in the end, probably thinking I was as drunk as they were.

Actually, thinking about it now, that may have helped!

At the time I started as a Constable I was nineteen years of age and was not allowed to go out in public until I was nineteen and a half years of age, which funnily enough was that Christmas Eve, so I was fairly excited when I was released onto the streets accompanied by older Officers initially to show me around.

I learnt very quickly that a lot of good Police work is down to sheer luck. I was on foot patrol one night with an older Officer who was showing me around Gateshead town shopping centre. He wasn't a very happy chap that night and made it very obvious with his one word answers to my questions and general silence in between. He had been taken off his car in order to show me how to carry out foot patrol duties and couldn't go for his usual nightshift refreshments.

It was about three o'clock in the morning and we were standing up an alley at the top of Jackson Street with our backs against a pair of solid wooden gates that was the entrance to the large Cooperative department store service road.

The little conversation we had had dried up and as we stood in the cold silence, a large cardboard box of cigarettes fell to the ground between us. We looked at each other, then looked up and saw a pair of legs dangling over the top of the gates. A guy dropped down between us facing the gate, looked either side and said, "SHIT!" My mate replied, "Yes son, and you're in it!"

My very first burglar had dropped from the sky straight into my arms!

I was with the same older Officer on another night when we heard a car door slam in the early hours of the morning as we walked the beat. We turned a corner and saw two lads abandoning what later turned out to be a stolen car. On seeing us they ran off and we gave chase. Well, I gave chase because the older Officer couldn't run for toffee.

As I ran after them towards the Tyne Bridge, I had my Police issue rubber torch in my hand and I threw the torch at one of the thieves. It bounced off his back into the road as he carried on unaffected. I then tripped over my torch and fell flat on the ground!

However, my body was pumping adrenaline and I didn't feel the pain until later. I immediately jumped back up and resumed the chase. I spotted a Sergeant off my shift ahead of us across the road and I shouted to him to stop them. He apprehended one of the thieves and as he did so, the older Officer ran up, grabbed the lad by the shoulder and said, "I've caught him, now get the other one!"

The Sergeant and I ran off in pursuit and we saw the thief drop down over a small wall at the foot of a grass embankment and crouch down completely still with his hands over his face.

It amazes me that people think they become invisible if they put their hands over their face like kids playing hide and seek.

We stopped directly above him and the Sergeant gave me a wink and a smile and said in a loud voice, "Well, it looks like we've lost him. I may as well have a piss while I'm here," and proceeded to pull up the front of his coat and pretend to pull down the zip of his fly. As he did so, the thief stood up with his hands in the air in a protective manner shouting, "Whoa, whoa, I'm here, don't piss on me!"

The older Officer and I got a commendation off the Chief Superintendent for that one.

The following year on New Year's Eve, I was doubled up with an Officer on foot patrol and we got a call to a distressed woman living on an estate at the back of the High Street. We attended the ground floor flat and were confronted at the door by a deaf and dumb woman who, it later transpired, had had an argument with her old man before he went off to the pub. She invited us in with hand signals and as we walked into the musty smelling living room, we saw the dining table laid out with glasses and a single bottle of Clan Dew, a mix of whiskey and wine.

The woman was obviously trying desperately to explain what had happened using a combination of grunts and hand signals but the other Officer answered with, "You what, do we want a drink, I'll not say no, ta," and grabbing two glasses, poured us a measure from the bottle. The woman continued to grunt and fling her arms around and as we finished off our drinks, the other Officer again said, "Do we want another drink, that's very kind pet, happy New Year," and again filled our glasses, raised them to her and swallowed. This happened three or four times until we nearly drank the bottle dry. By this time the woman was even more agitated and excited, but I think she had forgotten what her husband had done, her state was now down to the fact we had finished her only bottle.

We quickly departed with my colleague offering the all too common advice, "If he comes back and causes trouble, give us a ring."

I hate motorcycles. Always have. I've only been on one twice, and after the second occasion, I vowed never to mount one again, and so far, I've kept that vow.

I've attended too many fights between cars and motorcycles to know that the car nearly always wins.

The first occasion I boarded a motor cycle was when I was about nine years of age. It frightened the crap out of me.

The second occasion was just after I started the job and was allowed to patrol the streets alone. Someone told me we had the power to commandeer vehicles in emergencies, so one night while I was plodding the streets in the Bensham housing area, I received an intruder call not too far from my location. Occupants had disturbed a burglar breaking into their house.

As I received the call, I heard the roar of an engine approaching so I stepped into the road and flagged it down. A bloody motorcycle!

I explained to the rider that I needed to get to the far end of the estate as soon as possible and he indicated for me to jump on.

I don't know what it was, but this rider must have thought because he had a Policeman on board, he could break every road traffic law in the book. He revved so hard the tyres left scorch marks on the road and a cloud of blue smoke as we set off. He zoomed along the street at tremendous speed straight across every junction we came to without even slowing. My thighs were clamped hard against the sides and my fingernails must have left holes in the back of his jacket as I held on for dear life.

When he stopped at our destination, there was an overpowering smell of burning rubber. I was a nervous wreck and my legs were like jelly. I could hardly dismount for fear of them giving way under me. Luckily the burglar, who had probably heard us coming, was long gone, because believe me; I wouldn't have stood a remote chance of chasing or capturing him.

The Force Club Squad, which was responsible for licensed premises selling alcohol, used probationers to do plain clothed observations at pubs and clubs throughout the Northumbria area.

Perhaps it was because probationers didn't yet act or look like Police Officers, I don't know, but I got involved in a few jobs with them during my probation.

One job was at a pub on the outskirts of Sunderland. The pub had a late night refreshment extension which meant they could stay open an extra hour providing they served food.

The premises were dark and dismal with only the light from behind the bar illuminating the place. There was a kitchen accessed from behind the bar, and one night I asked the barman what food he could offer. He said, "Well, nothing really." I asked if he had any nuts or crisps and he replied, "No, but I can send someone around to the Chinese takeaway if you want!"

After a few weeks of observations, a raid was carried out and the matter later went to Court when we were all required to attend. One Officer, who had been in charge of the final raid, was in the witness box being grilled by the defence solicitor. Sometimes solicitors focused on a particular point of evidence but in doing so, forgot the obvious and this was a classic example.

The questioning went as follows;

"Officer, you have told the Court that you found no food at all on the premises."

"That's correct."

"And you said that you fully examined the kitchen behind the bar."

"That's correct."

"You also told the Court there were no lights in the kitchen."

"That's right Sir."

"Tell me Officer, did you have a torch?"

"No, I didn't."

"Did you have a cigarette lighter?"

"No, I didn't."

"Did you have any form of illumination on you?"

"No, I didn't."

"Then Officer, how can you say there was no food at all in the fridge?"

"Well, when I opened the fridge door, the little light came on!"

One smarmy solicitor shot down in flames.

There was a big Irish building site worker living in lodgings not far from Gateshead station and he spent his week working like a donkey and his weekends drinking like a fish.

He was as strong as an ox, built like a barn door and had a large beer belly that always hung over his trouser belt below his shirt.

He would return to his lodgings drunk as a skunk and work himself with his landlady, who would then call the Police. He never came quietly but usually, being so drunk, he wasn't too bad to handle.

One Friday night, the landlady made the call and I was delegated to attend. "Go on then young Shep, let's see what you can do with the Irishman," said the Sergeant as I walked out of the Police station doors.

I walked up Durham Road to the boarding house where I met the landlady standing with crossed arms at the front door. "He's upstairs in his room, I've had enough, I want him out," she said as I approached.

The house was a bit shabby with bits of wire and disused conduit pipes hanging from the ceiling, old worn wallpaper on the walls and no carpet on the stairs. Lodging houses weren't covered by the same laws as they are now.

I went up the stairs and saw the Irishman sitting on his bed with his head in his hands and obviously starting to feel the bad effects of drink.

"Come on mate, the landlady has had enough, you've got to go. You've went too far this time," I said to him while keeping my distance in case he fancied a fight. He looked over to me and surprisingly replied, "Aye, okay, no problem."

He pushed himself up off his bed and squeezed his huge bulk passed me as I let him go down the stairs first. I followed closely behind but did not see a bit of conduit pipe sticking out on the ceiling. The Irishman obviously knew about it and instinctively slightly ducked, but I didn't and it hit me dead centre of my forehead. I fell forward on top of the Irishman and we both rumbled down the stairs ending up in a heap at the bottom as the Irishman was screaming, "But I was coming quietly!"

When I later returned to the station, the Sergeant pointed to the swollen egg on my forehead shouting, "Ha, Shep's been chinned by the Irishman!"

Everyone had a favourite tea spot they would pop into for a chat and a cuppa. Tea spots were cultivated by various means and were a good place to hide from the Sergeant and have a cup of tea and rest. People were usually glad to see the Polis. I suppose it gave them a sense of security. It was also a good source of information about what was going on in the area.

Some tea spots were for individual Officers and their secrecy were fiercely protected by those Officers, but others were used by a number of Officers off different shifts. A favourite at the time was a self-service filling station at Bensham.

One of the lads on the shift attended the particular filling station after the girl on the till reported that a man had indecently exposed himself to her.

Apparently a car had pulled up at the far petrol pump from the garage shop, and the male driver while remaining seated in his car had indicated to the girl to approach him. She thought he was disabled and needed help to obtain petrol, so had left the till and approached the car. As she neared, the driver suddenly opened the car door, exposed himself towards her, shut the door and drove off.

The attending Officer took a statement from the victim and asked her, "Was the man sitting with an erection," and she replied, "No, it was a Ford Cortina - and he had a massive hard-on!"

There were a few of us who started on that shift about the same time and three of us teamed up on a social basis. I was the only one with a car and ferried the other two from pub to nightclub to home.

Sometimes we would finish work at 11pm, go nightclubbing and be back to work the next morning at 7am. When I think back now, I really don't know how the hell we did that. All part of being young and full of stamina I suppose.

One of the lads was always falling in love and getting engaged but the other lad and I did not mind as it gave us a good excuse to get him out and to help him drown his sorrows every time he broke his affair off.

On one occasion, the lad was particularly upset at finishing with a girl who was in the Specials, a voluntary team of uniformed civilians who helped us in simple duties such as events or traffic control, etc.

It was only later in the evening when the drink had loosened him up a bit that he confessed the reason for the break up. He had gone to bed with the particular female and had suggested doing it 'doggy style.' He explained he was behind her thrusting on the short strokes when she gasped, "Abdul used to like it like this," referring to a previous Arab boyfriend and oblivious to the fact that our colleague, for some reason, hated Arabs.

For the other lad and I that was funny enough but when we took our colleague to a nightclub that same night, the 'ex' was standing at the bar wrapping her arms and legs around a Detective Sergeant and tonguing the back of his throat, having gotten over her disengagement rather quickly.

Our colleague's eyes nearly popped out their sockets on seeing them and we had to pull him back out of the premises and visit another.

I walked the town centre beat and was covered by the town centre car driven by an older Officer, except on night shift when he was usually propping up the bar at a social club just off the High Street.

About 6am one morning just before we finished our shift, a member of the public approached me as I plodded the beat, and said one of my colleagues was parked up in his Police vehicle around the corner and he did not look too well. He suggested I check on him.

As I walked around, I saw the car parked at the kerb side with the Officer in the driver'sseat, fast asleep with his head pressed against the side window. I opened the door to check on him and he promptly fell out sprawling across the damp cold road. The impact on the cold wet surface brought him half to his senses as he jumped up, gave me a right mouthful, climbed back into the vehicle and went back to sleep.

The same Officer and I received a call one day that a man was sitting on the parapet of the Tyne Bridge with his legs dangling over the wrong side. We attended and saw the man on the west side. As we approached him he saw us and said, "Don't come any closer or I'll jump."

I've dealt with many suicide threats over the years and I know now that you can never tell if these people are bluffing and are just seeking attention, or if they are serious and they want someone to talk them out of it. The really serious ones just do it before anyone knows.

Nowadays, we would close the bridge off, have an ambulance on standby, request the Fire and Rescue Service to have their boat on the river, and have negotiators at the scene.

However, in the 1980's there was none of that and my colleague was not a man of patience.

We asked the man to get off the parapet but he refused so my colleague said, "Look, if you're going to jump, just do it instead of wasting our time, here, I'll help," and walked towards him with arms outstretched.

Luckily for him the man jumped off the parapet on the correct side and said, "You're fucking mad you, you were going to push me off!" My colleague said, "No, you're fucking mad, you were going to jump anyway!"

So the two of them stood arguing for a few minutes about who was madder until the man ran off towards Newcastle. Personally, I thought they were both bloody mad.

One of the lads who started about the same time as me, (I'll call him The Animal), and I used to work opposite beat patrols, he was covering West Street and I was covering the High Street. The streets were separated by a huge concrete mass of a shopping centre called Trinity Square, which had an ugly concrete structure of a multi storey car park towering above it. This was where part of the film 'Get Carter' starring Michael Caine was made.

On nightshift, The Animal and I would meet in Trinity Square for a chat and a smoke knowing that the patrolling Sergeant was unlikely to find us.

One night we heard the burglar alarm activate at a newsagents shop within the square and we ran down to find a large window smashed. We entered the premises through the jagged hole and checked the ground floor for the intruder.

We then proceeded to the only upper floor but could not find any lights. There were no windows and we had no torches.

The floor was used for storage and large boxes and display cards were piled high. Using the meagre light supplied from my cigarette lighter, we slowly and quietly walked the length of the room between the boxes, our sides touching, our ears craning for the slightest sound and our eyes straining through the darkness ahead of us.

Suddenly, the burglar stood up from amongst the boxes behind us with his hands held up and shouted, "Alright, you've got me, I'm here," as The Animal and I screamed and jumped into each other's arms.

After a late shift, we worked overtime on weekends on 'Team Patrol' when four or five of us would patrol in an enclosed Ford Transit van and respond to any fights or disorder reports.

We received a report one night of a fight at a fish and chip shop on the High Street.

By the time we attended the fight had ended and those involved had dispersed but, as we pulled up in the middle of the road, a heavily intoxicated guy who was munching away on a Chinese takeaway was walking across the road behind the van.

As The Animal burst open the back doors of the van, the door smacked the guy in the face sending his meal up in the air and splattering it all over the road. The guy looked at his meal, then at The Animal and screamed, "My fucking supper, look what you've done you stupid cunt." The Animal took hold of his collar, threw him into the back of the van and locked him up for being drunk and disorderly.

He was kept in overnight and put before the Magistrates the following morning when he pleaded guilty because he couldn't remember a single thing that had happened!

One of the Gateshead regular down and out drunks was arrested just about every day for minor offences. I'll call him Henry. His daily life entailed shoplifting, drinking and collapsing in that order.

His favourite brew was strong cider mixed with hair spray and boot polish. I don't know what it did, I never tried it. It must have given him one hell of a kick and knocked him out quicker.

I locked Henry up one day, I don't recall why, but when he'd sobered up, I took him into the fingerprint room, a small room attached to the main charge room within the cell area, to 'top and tail' him, (photograph and fingerprints).

As I was in the process, I heard the telephone ring in the charge room. I told Henry to wait and left the room to answer the phone.

I returned to the fingerprint room within a minute and a half to find Henry unconscious on the floor absolutely inebriated. Henry had drunk a full bottle of petrol that we used to clean the ink off the fingerprint pads.

That got Henry another five hours in the cells to sober up, and me a hefty verbal kicking up the rear off the Sergeant.

Sometimes probationers were moved about the Division they worked to get accustomed to the people and places. I was moved to the Birtley area on the outskirts of Gateshead on the Durham border for a short while, and dealt with my first two sudden deaths within a week of each other.

Okay, these incidents weren't 'har - har' funny. The first incident was more like - 'I don't believe it' kind of funny and the second was a 'what the hell' kind of funny.

The first was on a cold frosty morning when I had started at 6am and was walking along the deserted main street. I saw a man with a haversack on his back cycling towards me, obviously on his way to work. As he neared he said, "good morning," and I returned the greeting as he rode past. Within a second or so I heard a crash from behind, turned and saw the cyclist lying on the road next to his bike. It's strange the things that suddenly flash through your mind but my head was going left and right looking for a vehicle that might have hit him, but there was nothing or nobody in sight. I immediately ran up to the guy and found he was dead, just like that! Of course I later got the comments from my colleagues, 'It must have been the sight of you walking the beat!'

The second incident was on a Saturday afternoon when I was called to a sudden death in a public house on the main street of Birtley. The pub was busy and as I entered into the smoky noisy bar, I saw two ambulance men standing next to a group of three men sitting at a table playing dominoes. The body of an elderly man was lying under their table beside an empty chair.

I approached as the men continued to play dominoes. One of the ambulance men said to me, "He's dead," indicating to the body on the floor, and then one of the men sitting at the table holding his dominoes looked at me and said, "Aye, and I'm playing his hand and the lucky bugger would have won this game!"

It later transpired that the deceased had simply had a heart attack, perhaps brought on by the excitement of a game of dominoes.

The Animal and I were on the same driving course at Headquarters and our Instructor was a civilian who was from north of the borders.

Both being from Scotland, I expected The Animal and the Instructor to be clannish, but they hated each other for some reason from the very start, and I did not exactly hit it off well when the Instructor introduced himself and gave a short account of his background.

I recognised certain facts and asked if he had a son who used to attend my old school. When he confirmed my suspicions I said, "I was in the same class as him and in actual fact I blacked his eye on the last day we were at school," and he swung on me and said, "So it was you, you bastard, I remember that."

It was at that stage I realized that the guy had very little sense of humour.

That was the start of a wonderful driving course.

I think the real trouble started the day after when we were at Morpeth Police Station. It was a cold frosty morning, and the Instructor was hosing down the car. For some reason he suddenly thought it funny to turn the hose towards The Animal, splashing water over his uniform. However, vengeance was sweet and spontaneous.

I was driving that same morning towards Bellingham, a village in the heart of the Northumberland countryside. The Instructor was in the front passenger seat and The Animal was in the back. The Instructor was rolling his own cigarette looking down at his work with the tobacco box nestled on his knees. As I drove along the narrow country road, I swear to this day, a rabbit suddenly shot out from the grass verge and I jammed the brakes on causing his tobacco box to fall and spill the contents into the foot well.

"What the fuck are you doing," shouted the Instructor.

"A rabbit shot out in front of me," I replied.

"Fuck the rabbit, get in the back. You, take over."

The Animal and I exchanged places, and as we passed each other outside the car, he gave me a little smile and winked.

We set off again and the Instructor resumed preparing his cigarette having recovered the spillage. He put the creation into his mouth, took out the glowing car cigarette lighter and as he put it near the end of the cigarette,

The Animal suddenly banged on the brakes causing the cigarette lighter to jab the end of the Instructors nose.

The car was filled with loud cries of pain and obscenities as The Animal and I tried to stifle our laughter with hands over our mouths.

The Instructor displayed a huge blister on the end of his nose for the remainder of our course but must have realized he had been beaten because he never tried to get us back.

A great guy worked at Felling Police Station not too far from Gateshead. He was a giant of a man, built like a brick shit house but, as I later discovered, he was a gentle giant if you kept yourself in his good books. His wife was tiny in comparison but was obviously the dominant of the pairing.

I was courting a Policewoman from my shift at the time and on New Year'sEve; we were at a party at a public house at Heworth. We were sitting at a long table in company of about a dozen people. The giant sat to my right opposite my girlfriend and I sat next to him directly opposite his wife.

As the evening progressed and the ale flowed more easily, I was encouraged to tell a joke. I stood up and told about a tiny baldy man standing at a bar having a pint when he was approached by a giant muscular bigheaded guy. The athlete looked the little man up and down and sneeringly tutted and said, "Look at you, you're skinny and a poor example of what a real man should be like. I am handsome, muscular, athletic and a prime example of how a real man should be."

The little man looked at the giant and said, "Yes, but I've got something you haven't got, I've got this!" I pulled down my trouser zip to gasps from the female audience, reached inside my fly and pulled out the bottom front tail of my shirt saying, "I've got a longer shirt tail than you!"

Everybody burst out laughing as I pulled my zip back up and resumed my sitting position. I took a large mouthful of ale and as I did so, the giant turned to me, stifling his laughter and said, "Fuck me, I thought you were going to get your cock out!"

I couldn't hold the mouthful of ale as my cheeks expanded in an effort to hold my laugh and a spray of pressurized golden lager shot out showering his wife directly in her face.

As she sat in dripping disbelief, my life flashed before my eyes thinking her husband would kill me and as I turned and apologized, he was laughing even harder with tears rolling down his face saying, "No, no, that was funnier than the fucking joke!"

Another thing I learned in the job at a very early stage was to never expose your weaknesses for fear of long lasting piss taking, and when I say long lasting, some people never forget things for the rest of your service.

One Officer on the shift had a couple of years more service than I, and it was during my probation that I found out about his secret fear.

We were doubled up one nightshift and I was driving. It was in the early hours of the morning and the radio was quiet. My colleague was sitting low in the front passenger seat and was trying to catch some sleep. I drove into Hawks Road on the outskirts of Gateshead town centre to an abattoir. At the entrance there was a big open unlit shed where they piled all the animal skins and it was usually running with rats, especially at that time in the morning. I drove in the shed and saw rats the size of cats running in all directions, and as I muttered, "Bloody hell," under my breath at the sight of them, my colleague opened his eyes. Within a fraction of a second, he realized where he was and caught sight of the scurrying brown bodies. He screamed like a woman, grabbed me by the left shoulder and shouted "GET ME OUT OF HERE, GET ME OUT OF HERE."

As I reversed from the darkness of the shed, he had sunk even lower in his seat, pale faced and shivering at the sight of his dreaded fear, RATS!

I don't know how the rest of the shift found out about this. Perhaps I may have uttered something to someone in confidence but for months after, my poor colleague suffered jokes about rats, rat references, squeaking noises as people walked past and rat cartoons

drawn in his pocket note book.

Sometimes, in particular on nightshifts when things are quiet and you want something to happen, you can get a little too eager and discretion is no longer a consideration.

Towards the end of my two year probationary period, I was on nightshift when one of our Sergeants on the shift shouted for assistance on his radio from the High Street just after midnight.

We all attended with blue lights flashing and saw the Sergeant standing next to an automatic pedestrian crossing at the junction with Park Lane. Three guys were standing a few yards from him.

As we jumped out of the cars, the Sergeant pointed at the three guys and in a highly excited angry state shouted, "Arrest them three, lock them up."

We grabbed the three guys who immediately protested their innocence saying, "We've done nowt, what have we done?" I turned to the Sergeant and said, "What are they locked up for sarge?" He replied, "They pressed the pelican crossing and didn't use it!"

In total disbelief because what they did wasn't even an offence, I said, "Hey sarge, I know I'm still in my probation but.......fuck off man!"

As the Sergeants face turned red and steam erupted from his ear holes, I sent the three guys on their way.

I had to stay out of the Sergeants way for a few nights after that until he cooled down!

CHAPTER 2
FULLY FLEDGED. I'M A REAL POLICEMAN.

A 1970's cap badge. I preferred caps to helmets. People didn't call you 'tithead'. They still called you 'black bastard' and 'pig' but not 'tithead'.

One of the colourful characters on the shift was nicknamed 'Shipwreck' because that was exactly what he always looked like.

He had a craggy face that was twenty years older than his actual age, his nostrils and ears sprouted wiry hair and his face always had two days of beard growth.

He never pressed his uniform or polished his shoes or combed his hair.

Shipwreck used to roll his own cigarettes and when he was driving, he would have the car heater fan blowing full blast and he would just flick his cigarette ash as his hand held the steering wheel. Shipwreck could never understand the purpose of an ashtray. His car was like one of those ornamental globes that showed a snow scene when you shook it. As he stepped out of the car and walked away, there was a trail of very fine white cigarette ash coming from his speckled uniform.

I used to hate being doubled up with Shipwreck because your black uniform would be speckled from top to bottom and you looked as though you had the worst case of dandruff ever. On returning to the station, other Officers would look at you, shake their heads sympathetically and say, "Been with Shipwreck eh?"

But, just like most of the other guys on the shift, he was a likeable man who would help you if he could.

Big E. was another giant of a character who worked in the front office at Gateshead on my shift. He had a shiny baldy head and a permanent smile that always stretched from ear to ear. It was said that you could hear his laugh on all five floors of the station. Big E. was the biggest character of all working in Northumbria Police at the time.

He was working front office permanently for a reason.

When I first started at Gateshead, Big E. was the town centre car driver and one night he was patrolling alone when he visited a public house at Hawks Road just on the outskirts of the town centre, as he had heard a new Manager had taken over. Big E. thought he would introduce himself and get a free pint in the process.

The premises had two doors at the front leading into the one roomed bar, and as Big E. entered the premises, he saw two men rolling about the floor fighting. Big E. calmly approached them, picked one up by the front of his jacket, smacked him one and threw him out into the street. As he re-entered, the second man made good his escape through the other door.

Thinking this enjoyable task was definitely worth a free pint, Big E. approached the barmaid and asked if the new Manager was about, and the barmaid informed him he had just thrown the new Manager into the street!

Hence, Big E. wasn't allowed back on the streets.

One thing the young lads and lasses on the shift learnt was never to leave your refreshments around where Big E. could find it, because you could bet your last penny, it wouldn't be there for long.

I mistakenly left my sandwich in the front office once and when I returned for it, Big E. was sitting with a big smile on his face with the empty packet in front of him and he said to me, "Tell Mrs. Shepherd (my mother) she makes lovely sandwiches!"

He did not give two hoots about anything or what anyone thought but, as with most of the characters on the shift, he was a likeable man and such a good laugh. You just couldn't fall out with Big E.

Big E. liked to do a spot of sea fishing on his days off and one time, he had returned to the harbour after a day out and was walking along a jetty.

He noticed two young lads aged about ten years sitting at the edge of the jetty fishing off the side with harbour reels.

As he walked towards them, he saw three older skinhead types approach the young lads and one of the skinheads kicked their fishing gear and bags over the side into the sea about ten feet below.

Big E. was furious and dropping his kit, he ran up to the offending skinhead, grabbed him by the collar and threw him straight over the side into the sea without hesitation or consideration as to whether the skinhead could swim or not, (luckily, he could - or he learned very quickly).

As the other two skinheads ran off, Big E. handed enough money to the shocked boys to buy new harbour reels.

That was Big E's answer of instant justice and compensation.

We were working night shift one New Year's Eve and in the morning as our shift ended, one of our colleagues invited everyone back to his house for a drink including Big E. Big mistake!

These were unknown arrangements to our colleague's wife who, as we entered the front door, appeared at the top of the stairs in a white see-through negligee.

Of course Big E. had to spoil the occasion by pointing and shouting out at the sight of her, "I can see your wife's little fanny," in a melodious voice that carried three houses either side.

Big E. used to get the car drivers to buy a couple of bottles of brown ale from the off licence at the start of night shift, which he secreted in his drawer in the front office so he could take regular gulps during the night.

One night, two of the lads got Big E's refreshments which they put on the back seat of the Police car. As they were returning to the station, they spotted a stolen car containing two young lads being driven along Prince Consort Road just up the street from the station.

They gave chase but the thieves panicked and did a handbrake spin in front of the Police car, which then went straight into the side of the stolen vehicle.

On impact, the bottles of brown ale flew past the heads of the two Officers and smashed all over the dashboard.

Big E. had been listening to the commotion over the radio and ran out of the station and up the street to the crash. He ignored the two dazed Officers as they climbed out of the wrecked Police car, pulled open the door of the stolen car, grabbed the two occupants and started shouting, "You little bastards, you've smashed me beer!"

A lazy sod sometimes worked the control room, which was on what we called ground level but was actually raised one floor above the surrounding streets. The windows ran the full length of the room and overlooked the rear yard.

A Superintendent entered the Control Room early one morning and, looking around, he said, "Look at the state of this place, all these dirty cups lying about. Get rid of these cups."

Lazy Sod replied, "What would you like me to do with them Boss?" The Superintendent said, "I don't care, just get rid of them," whereupon Lazy Sod piled the twenty or so cups on a tray, opened the window and threw the lot out as the Superintendent stood with eyes and mouth wide at the sound of the crashing crockery in the yard below.

I was with Lazy Sod one late shift working the Low Fell area car when we got an intruder call to a launderette in the Beacon Lough area just before we were due to finish our shift. This will explain why I nicknamed him Lazy Sod.

When we arrived, the female key holder was standing outside the locked premises and a young lad was trapped inside peering out through the glass door.

Apparently the lad had burgled the premises by dropping through a skylight on the roof but having done so then found he was unable to climb back up. He obviously hadn't thought it through.

The key holder unlocked the door and as we entered the premises, Lazy Sod took hold of the lad and said, "What are you doing in here son?" and the lad replied, "Screwing the place."

I was impressed. It looked like Lazy Sod was going to make an arrest.

However, a straight cough was not going to put Lazy Sod off from cuffing an arrest and he said, "Look, if I let you go, do you promise not to do this again."

The key holder looked at me and I looked at Lazy Sod expecting him to say, "Only kidding, you're under arrest," but it never came so I had to jump in and take over the arrest. The lazy sod!

I was the town centre panda driver one early shift and went out patrolling alone at 6.15am.

I drove to an area by the river Tyne known locally as 'The Bunk' where stolen vehicles were frequently abandoned.

As I drove down the hill, I spotted a car parked up at the far end of the waste ground and thought, 'here we go, probably a stolen car.'

However, as I drove nearer, I could see a man in the driver's seat and a woman in the front passenger seat both fast asleep. I approached and knocked on the window, awakening the two occupants.

The man wound down his window and I said, "Everything alright?"

The man looked at me with half closed eyes and said, "What time is it like?"

I looked at my watch and replied, "Six thirty."

There was a slight pause as he took the information in and then his eyes widened, he shot upright in his seat and shouted, "Fuck me, the wife will kill me!"

He shouted at his passenger to wake up, reached over to pull her door open and pushed her out sprawling her on all fours in the wet grass. He then drove off at speed leaving me to take a used, abused and very tearful girl home.

One of the characters on our shift was the shift ram. Women seemed to adore him. I never found out why because he was overweight and ugly, but a hell of a good laugh.

He treated his wife like crap and even charged her rent for their Police house they lived in.

She must have been the only Police wife in the country who did not know that Police accommodation was free.

The Ram had been getting away with this scam for about two years but his greed got the better of him.

One day, he told her that the rent had gone up but she need not worry, he would just pay it as usual. Then he would give her his pay packet minus the rent, which was a handy monthly allowance for The Ram to spend on other female companions.

His wife went to a local Police club one night and mentioned to the other wives present that it was terrible the Force had increased the rent for the Police houses, resulting in fits of giggles and laughter from the assembled audience.

The facts were exposed to her and The Ram later got his pockets emptied and a burnt lug hole.

The Ram lived in a cul de sac at the back of Whickham Police Station, and one of his neighbours was also on our shift.

The Ram saw his colleague's wife in the street one day and for a laugh said to her, "Has he bought you a present with his winnings then," giving her a wink.

"What do you mean," she enquired.

"You know, when he won the bandit at the Police club the other night," he said.

She still played ignorant.

"EE, I shouldn't have said nowt, I bet he's getting a surprise for you," The Ram said and walked off.

His neighbour immediately went into the house and confronted her husband.

He obviously did not know what she was talking about and denied everything.

"You're lying," she said, "I'll find it if I have to turn the house upside down," and commenced a house search the Drug Squad would have been proud of.

It just so happened that her husband kept a little nest egg in a shoe under the fridge, which she found and confiscated under the impression that The Ram had been truthful about her husband's luck.

I enjoyed working with The Ram; as he was such a great laugh all of the time. I remember in February 1979, we had terrific snow storms and freezing climates. The Ram acquired a table tennis ball which he cut a hole in and painted red. He walked about his beat popping into shops and approaching people at bus stops wearing the table tennis ball on his nose and saying, "It's bloody freezing isn't it?"

We worked together at Birtley office, a sub section about six miles from Gateshead main station.

Our Sergeant was known as Budgie, the reason for which will be explained later.

Birtley office was a transformed house with the uniformed Officers rooms downstairs and the C. I. D. upstairs. Our radios were kept in a very small, unlit walk-in cupboard that had a shelf facing you as you opened the door.

One night shift, The Ram and I found a cat which had been recently killed on the road. Rigor Mortis had set in and The Ram picked it up and took it back to the office.

He set it up on the back shelf of the radio cupboard with a paw raised in the air and a snarled look on its face, a setup for the Sergeant as he always checked the radios at refreshment time.

We then retired to the rest room and waited for Budgie the Sergeant.

A few minutes later we heard the back door open and footsteps proceed down the passageway. Then we heard the radio cupboard door open followed swiftly with a scream and the sound of furniture being knocked over.

The Ram and I looked at each other, both recognizing that the screams did not belong to our Sergeant.

We ran through to find our other colleague lying on his back amongst tumbled chairs, eyes wide and complexion pale. We quickly helped him to his feet and rushed him through to the rest room knowing Budgie was due any second.

We had to muffle our laughter and stifle our colleague's verbal obscenities as we again heard the back door open, footsteps proceed down the corridor and the squeak of the radio cupboard door followed by screams of, "You bastards," from the right target.

The Ram was acting up in the rank of Sergeant and over the period of a week or so, he had upset one or two of the lads with his 'holier than thou' attitude. He used to travel to Birtley office on a small motorbike and one nightshift we, I mean someone, stuck a piece of paper with 'CUNT HEAD' written on just above the visor of his motorcycle helmet.

I know, pretty childish but funny all the same.

To be honest, we, I mean the culprit expected him to notice but at the end of our shift, he did not see the piece of paper as he put the helmet on. Unknown to us or the culprit, he then went to a local hospital where his wife worked to give her a lift home. He happily walked the miles of corridors of the hospital with a big smile on his face while wearing the helmet, wondering what everyone was looking at and receiving no replies to his "good morning" greetings.

Apparently, on seeing the notice his wife pointed at it and said, "They got that right didn't they!"

Our Sergeant, Budgie, was so called due to his hobby of budgerigar keeping and his continuous conversations on the subject. Pretty obvious wasn't it. Budgie very rarely took off his Police helmet as he was bald on top but grew his side hair long and wrapped it around his dome in an attempt to look dignified. However, he was oblivious to the fact he looked ridiculous sitting very low in a Ford Escort panda car wearing his helmet.

He had a particular dialect and referred to everyone as 'young'un'.

The Animal was working with him at Birtley one Sunday and Budgie enquired what he was doing that day. Sundays were very quiet then as nearly all of the shops were closed and were ideal days to catch up on paperwork.

The Animal told him he was going to get a statement from someone regarding a road traffic accident.

"I've got nowt to do young'un, I'll come with you," said Budgie following The Animal out to the Police vehicle.

The Animal wasn't too pleased about this and raised his eyes and gave a loud groan as they drove off.

On arrival, they were invited in by the occupant.

Budgies eyes lit up as he walked into the sitting room and was faced with a beautiful coloured bird in a cage. He examined the bird carefully with his face up against the bars as The Animal tried to ignore him and got on with the statement.

"Hey young'un, you know, this birds beak is too long, it needs trimmed back," said Budgie to the owner, "If you get 'is a pair of nail scissors young'un, I'll do it for you now."

Armed with the said tools, Budgie grabbed the defenceless bird in one fist and commenced the operation.

A few minutes later he returned the bird to its cage with blood leaking from the shortened beak, and in full view of the owner, it promptly fell off its perch and lay motionless on the sandpaper floor. "Don't worry young'un, it's just a bit dazed, it'll be alright in a minute," Budgie advised as The Animal made his excuses and dragged him away from the house having completed the statement.

About an hour later a very upset ex-budgie owner rang Birtley office to say a Sergeant had killed his prized pet, which resulted in everyone on the shift donating towards the cost of a new one.

One of the lads working Birtley office was still in his probation.

He was somewhat over weight. Well, excessively fat really. One night, he was waddling along the High Street when a drunk on the opposite side started shouting, "Hoy, fatty, you couldn't catch me if you tried."

The probationer told him to piss off or he would arrest him but the drunk was game for a chase.

After several warnings, (because he had doubts whether he could catch him or not), the probationer eventually ran over the road.

The drunk ran off along the footpath swerving from side to side chased by the fat probationer. As the probationer got within reaching distance, he suddenly dived towards the drunk but missed and went straight through the back windscreen of a parked car.

The drunk made good his escape.

Luckily, the probationer was uninjured, but obviously very embarrassed. He spent the next day writing reports as to why Northumbria Police were faced with a bill for a new car windscreen.

A new lad who was an ex-Navy man joined our shift, and one night when we were off duty, we were having a few pints in Gateshead Police club for a celebration, when he suggested we play 'pass the parcel' to liven the evening up. We agreed and he went off to the toilets for a few minutes to prepare the parcel.

On his return he had a large newspaper wrapped parcel and we sat around in a circle as the barmaid switched the piped music on and off.

The parcel was passed from one person to the next and each time the music stopped, a layer of paper was stripped from the parcel by whoever was holding it at that time.

However, as the paper was stripped of a layer of paper, it became apparent to everyone that the parcel was getting warmer and damper and everyone started to look at each other nervously. The parcel was getting passed to each other quicker and quicker until someone couldn't take any more and suddenly shouted, "I know what it is you dirty bastard," and threw the parcel at the ex-Navy lad. He caught it, stripped the last few layers of paper off and revealed a hot face cloth! Everyone burst out laughing and had obviously been thinking along the same lines. It just showed the power of the collective imagination.

I was sent to a neighbourly dispute at the Bensham area of Gateshead, where a young couple complained that the friendly resident above them had put shit all over their back windows.

On examining the evidence it appeared that human excreta had been thrown at the two back windows. There was quite a lot and the stench was unbelievable.

I arrested the man for conduct likely to cause a breach of the peace and he fully admitted he had shit in a bucket for a week then thrown the collection over the neighbour's property as he was in dispute with them over noise.

He asked to see his Solicitor who duly turned out and spoke to the client in private. The Solicitor then left the station and I asked the man what his Solicitor had advised.

The man said, "He told me I should have done a good job of it and thrown it over the bastards head."

I said, "Is that right," and immediately wrote the conversation in my pocket book, which he then signed.

It later went to Court and as I was giving evidence, the same Solicitor was trying to be clever by asking why I didn't seize the bucket as evidence.

I told the Court I didn't think they would want to face the evidence after three months, and the Magistrates whispered to each other and agreed with obvious expressions of relief on their face.

The solicitor then asked to see my pocket book and I handed it over with a wry grin on my face. He read the book for all of two seconds, paled and stammered, "No more questions," then quickly planted his bottom down. Needless to say, the case was proved and the Solicitor disappeared from the building rather quick.

A young lady reported concern for her disabled parents who resided together in a ground floor flat. I attended and spoke to the girl outside the premises. She told me that her parents never leave the house and she couldn't get an answer at the door. She was very concerned that something had happened to them. We tried banging on the doors and windows, shouting through the letterbox and ringing them on the telephone, all to no avail.

Because of the concern, I decided to kick open the front door. I wasn't aware at that time that just inside the door was an inner full glass door. As I kicked open the door, the air pressure between the two doors smashed the glass of the second door, and just as that happened, the girl said, "Here's my parents now."

I looked up the street to see an elderly man pushing his wife down the footpath in a wheelchair.

The girl ran up to them saying, "Where have you been, I've been worried," and then burst into tears, pointed to me and said, "And he's just smashed your door!"

I thought, "What! Well thanks for that. Bitch."

Thank God I had had the sense to get her to sign my pocket book giving permission before the deed was carried out.

I did my Criminal Investigation Department Aids, a preparatory course prior to being accepted for C. I. D. at Newburn which was about 6 miles from Gateshead. I thought at the time that my placing was a little unfair as I was the only one who didn't do the course at their home station.

The positive side of it was that Newburn covered part of the Scotswood area, which I grew up in. The negative side was that I was dealing with people I went to school with.

One Sunday morning, I reported for duty at Newburn and was asked immediately if I could fingerprint a prisoner who had been arrested the night before for stealing a car.

I went through to the charge room to be faced with my relative who was sporting a black eye, bent nose and bruised chin.

Slightly shocked, but not a lot as he was known by the family to be a dodgy character anyway, I asked what had happened.

He replied, "I pinched this blokes car last night but as I drove out of the street, a guy waved his arms and flagged me down. I thought he was in trouble so I stopped but it was the owner of the car."

"So he did all that," I asked pointing to the injuries on his face.

"Well, he did me eye and me nose, but the Polis bopped me chin," he said.

"What for," I asked puzzled and he replied, "Well, when they put me in the back of the panda, I saw this torch lying on the back seat and I thought that's a canny torch and stuffed it in my jacket. The Policeman wasn't happy when he searched me at the Police station and found his own torch!"

Needless to say he completely failed his criminal activities examination that night and was never going to be a criminal mastermind.

When I first started the job, the pay was abysmal, so the people who applied to join the Police Force then actually wanted to be Police Officers. It wasn't until the mid-eighties when the pay and conditions got a lot better.

At the same time, major changes were taking place. Boundaries were changing within the Force area, Stations lost their own control rooms to two main control rooms, one south of the river Tyne and one to the north, and we were becoming computerised.

Previously, the areas covered by each station were called Divisions. There was Gateshead Division, Newcastle Division, Sunderland Division, etc.

But as the changes were taking place, some bright spark decided that the areas should be called Command Units. There was Command Unit Gateshead, Command Unit Newcastle, Command Unit Sunderland, etc.

However, Command Unit North Tyneside did not like their abbreviation and so the titles had to be quickly changed to Area Commands.

I worked for a few years at Low Fell, a district of Gateshead about two miles from the main station.

I worked with a great guy who had a fiery temper and because of it, was nicknamed Tiger.

We received a call one day of a domestic situation and attended a small stone built cottage just off the main road.

On arrival, we were invited in and spoke to the female occupant who explained that her husband had bought a new pair of black shoes a few days previously, which he left just inside the front door. On this particular day of our attendance, he had gone out drinking and on returning home in an inebriated state, he spotted the shoes in the passage and for some reason, thought they were someone else's shoes and accused his wife of having an affair with a 'black' man.

As she was explaining this to us, the sitting room door suddenly burst open and in walked her totally naked husband covered from head to foot in black boot polish and shouting, "So you want a fucking black man, well here's a fucking black man!"

We didn't really want to touch him, firstly because he was naked and secondly, in fear of getting covered in polish. However, we had no choice and he was arrested and kept in for Court the following morning.

He still had the black polish all over himself when he appeared before the Court, fully clothed I should add.

He ended up getting a slap on the wrist and released. I think the Magistrates took a shine to him!

Tiger used to tell me often that the only time he was ever disciplined in the job was when an Inspector, who had retired long before my time, caught him one nightshift in a Police box having a cup of tea.

Apparently, the Inspector took exception to the fact that Tiger was not patrolling the streets, and had rapped on the Police box with his fist shouting, "Come on now Officer, I know you're in there."

Tiger was fined £5 by the Chief Constable, a lot of money in those days for such a minor matter.

The retired Inspector lived at Low Fell, and whenever we saw him, Tiger would point and say, "There's the bastard that cost me a fiver."

If any ex-Police Officers who resided in our area died, on duty Officers were delegated to pall bear.

Usually, four Officers would attend the deceased's house and carry the coffin into the hearse, and then attend the cemetery or crematoria and carry the coffin to its final destination.

I used to hate the job because you always got covered in sawdust from the bottom of the coffin on your black uniform and it took days to get rid of it.

When the ex-Inspector in question died, I was surprised that Tiger volunteered to pall bear.

On the day, four of us attended the house, and as the family and relatives were being ushered to the waiting funeral cars, we were shown into the sitting room where the coffin was positioned on a trestle in the centre of the room.

As soon as Tiger entered the room, he went straight up to the coffin, rapped on the lid with his fist and said, "Come on now Inspector, I know you're in there!"

We loaded the coffin into the hearse, then jumped back into the Police van and sped down to the crematoria. We just pulled up and saw a hearse coming up the drive.

I remember saying to the others at the time, "Bloody hell, they were quick."

As soon as it stopped, we unloaded the coffin onto our shoulders, and slowly walked into the church.

We then stood at the back as the service began, but a few minutes later, our shift Inspector suddenly ran in and whispered to us as he pointed outside, "What are you's doing in here, the coffin has just arrived!"

Whoever's funeral it was got a very nice sendoff but the mourners must have been wondering what the hell was going on.

I did a dog suitability course with a view to joining the Dog Section, and spent two weeks just before Christmas at Police Headquarters.

The course was designed to test you to possibly becoming a dog handler. At that time, they were in the process of training specialized dogs to sniff out bodies, drugs and explosives. The body dog was trained to detect human blood and our course training Sergeant was in charge of that particular dog.

One day, the Sergeant decided to take the dog up into the hills with us to give it a bit training, and probably show off to us.

We put the dog in the back of the van and went to the hospital where the Sergeant obtained a steel lid-topped bucket full of blood and bits.

He put it into the back of the van with the dog and we travelled up to Harwood Forest in the wilds of Northumberland. When we went to get the dog out of the back, the Sergeant opened the back doors and we were faced with blood everywhere, the bucket lying on its side and the dog licking its bloody smiling face!

Years later I was obtaining a statement from an elderly couple and they happened to mention they loved Police dogs. They told me they went to all the country fairs just to see them jumping over obstacles and through blazing hoops. I told them I had a story about Police dogs and commenced telling them about the dog trained to detect dead bodies.

At the end I was laughing my head off but realized that the elderly couple was sitting in silence with eyes and mouths agape in total shock.

Sometimes I forgot I was talking to ordinary members of the public who didn't have a clue about Police matters.

I wouldn't be surprised if that poor couple never attended a Police dog exhibition again!

While on the course, we heard of an embarrassing incident with the explosives trained dog. A suspicious package was reported as having been found lying in a shop doorway in Sunderland. The package was left in place, the street was cordoned off and the new explosives trained dog was called for, as it was considered a perfect scenario to try the dog out, the first time in a real incident.

In view of a mass of public spectators, the dog handler stood behind the barriers with other Officers about 200 yards from the package. The dog approached in a perfect straight line as ordered and sniffed at the package.

Now, at this point, if the package contained explosives, the dog was trained to give a signal. It was supposed to stand on its back legs, wave its front paws in the air and bark, IT'S A FUCKING BOMB!"

I'm only joking. It was supposed to bark, simple as that. But this dog completely forgot its training, picked up the package in its teeth and merrily trotted back towards the handler. As the other Officers were taking several steps backwards, the handler was frantically waving his hands in the air and shouting, "DROP, - STOP, - DOWN, - BAD BOY!" much to the amusement of the gathered crowd.

I was amazed to see that the training staff wore old uniform jackets while training the dogs to attack. Runners wearing padded leather sleeves on one arm over the uniform jackets ran ahead of the dog and when the runner was about 200 yards away, the handler released the dog to catch the runner. As the dog approached, the runner turned towards it and as it jumped, he fed the sleeved arm into its mouth. The handler would then approach and instruct the dog to release.

So, we basically had a load of Police dogs trained to attack anything that looked like a Police Officer.

I ran for a couple of dogs while on the course and there was one particular dog that was a real sly bastard with jaws like vice grips.

This devious sod ran after me one day and as it jumped, I fed my padded sleeve into its mouth but as it gripped, its teeth slid along the sleeve and the momentum carried the dog off and past me. Undeterred, it suddenly swung round and jumped again but this time I fed the wrong arm into its mouth and I thought it was going to break my bones. Luckily I was wearing a thick lumberjack jacket and only suffered a lot of pain and bruising. That dog learned a few choice profanities that day.

The Sergeant in charge of our course was a hard country raised man brought up in the wildest parts of Northumberland. He was a likeable man but had an annoying habit which we tried to cure.

Each morning everyone on the course was given a packed lunch to take with us. At dinnertime, we would get our lunches out and start eating. However, the Sergeant never brought any and would just sit watching us. Feeling sorry for him, someone would offer a sandwich, someone else an apple and another person would give him a packet of crisps. This happened just about every day and the wily fox used to end up with more fodder than anyone.

Towards the end of the course, we decided to set him up. We prepared a sandwich with pepper, curry powder, chilli powder and mustard. This sandwich was on fire!

We sat in amazement when the bastard ate the whole lot and never said a word.

On the last day he got his own back. He arranged for us to be transported to a pub at dinnertime for a farewell pint, saying he would meet us there. The pub was about six miles from headquarters where our cars were. Of course, we received a phone call from him saying he couldn't meet us and we had to make our own way back. It was a freezing day with thick snow on the roads. We started walking but after a couple of miles, we managed to hitch a lift the rest of the way, so it wasn't as bad as he expected.

CHAPTER 3
C. I. D.

A 1980's cap badge. Helmets had their advantages. You could keep your fish and chips in them and keep your head warm at the same time.

During my three years in the Criminal Investigation Department at Gateshead from 1982, I experienced some of the funniest incidents I ever witnessed in my career.

One in particular was when I was working with a guy who had the deepest voice in the Force and probably one of the driest humours.

We had arrested a man for something and were in the process of interviewing him.

In those days, we used to write down all the questions and replies and then get the prisoner to read over and endorse the record.

We were just completing the interview process and I was tidying up the record of interview as my colleague, who was sitting next to me opposite the prisoner, completed a descriptive form which gives details of a person's physical description and mannerisms.

My colleague was hunched over the form with his head down and without looking up, he asked, "What colour are your eyes?"

There was silence from the prisoner and when I looked up I saw him sitting with his hands over his eyes. Still without looking up, my colleague repeated the question and the prisoner remained with his hands over his eyes completely silent.

Again, he repeated the question and the prisoner remained in the same position.

This time my colleague looked up and aggressively asked, "WHAT COLOUR ARE YOUR EYES?"

The prisoner took his hands away from his face and said, "Ar, I thought you said cover your eyes."

My colleague said, "What the fuck did you think I was going to do, kiss you!"

I was renowned for my jokes and could rattle them off one after the other.

The female station cleaners were always asking me to tell them one, and one morning one of the cleaners and her pal approached me with a joke request.

I said, "There was a little lad on a bus with his mother and he was crying his eyes out. His mother asked what was wrong and the little lad bawled I've lost my little green ball. His mother said don't worry son, I'll find it and bent down to check the floor.

Ten minutes later, the lad looked around and saw everyone on the bus bending down. He asked his mother what all the people were doing and she said they're looking for your little green ball son. The lad said tell them not to bother, I'll make another one, and stuck a finger up his nose."

As I did the action, one of the cleaners put a hand to her mouth and with eyes wide, suddenly ran off towards the toilets.

The other cleaner turned to me and said, "She's a bit cockily with jokes like that. Talk about sick, shit or snots and she's off. It's since last week when we were shopping. This old man was walking towards us and spat a big green one out on the path in front of us. She was at the kerb being sick for fifteen minutes."

About half an hour later I saw her pal and I said, "Hey, I'm sorry about before," and she said, "Oh it's alright, I enjoy a joke, it's just last week we were shopping when this old man...."

I quickly interrupted with, "I know, your friend told me," but she continued with the story.

As she neared the end her eyes opened wide, her hand went to her mouth and she was off to the toilet like a vomiting hare.

When I returned to the C. I. D. office, I spoke to a colleague and told him what had happened. Now this particular colleague was well known for his obnoxious farts and I'll refer to him as Farty Pants. I warned him not to drop one in front of that particular cleaner.

At dinnertime, Farty Pants went up to the canteen on the top floor and came back down by the lift.

As he did so, he let one rip in the lift and when the doors opened, who should be standing there, but the very same cleaner.

Remembering what I said, Farty Pants warned her someone had farted in the lift and she said, "Get away, you're kidding me," and stepped in.

Her eyes went wide, her hand went over her mouth and she was off.

As I said, Farty Pants was renowned for his obnoxious farts and could easily clear an office within seconds of dropping one.

He was usually doubled up with another particular Detective and on one occasion, they were driving in Newcastle City centre and stopped at traffic lights.

As they waited for the lights to change, Farty Pants, who was in the passenger seat, let blast. His colleague jumped out of the driver's seat and stood at the side of the car in the middle of the road shouting into the open door, "You dirty stinking bastard."

Farty Pants suddenly jumped into the driver's seat, slammed the door shut and drove off leaving his colleague in the street and causing him to have to get a bus back to Gateshead.

Earlier, I mentioned that a lot of good Police work is down to pure luck. Sometimes you just walked around the corner and find yourself faced with burglars or car thieves. Sometimes, you had to be a little bit cheeky.

Farty Pants was dealing with a burglary of a house where a television had been stolen. The night after it happened, we went to a local public house where Farty Pants spoke to one of the bar maids.

He mentioned about the burglary and asked if she had heard anything about it. She said, "No, but there's a lad who lives just down the street from my mother and he's a burglar. Everybody knows him." We obtained the address and decided to give it a visit.

A man answered the door and we immediately recognized him as he had 'assisted the Police with their enquiries' a number of times before. Farty Pants said, "Hello mate, we've come about the burglary from last night," and pushed past the shocked occupant into the downstairs flat.

The man followed saying, "What burglary? I don't know what you're talking about." Farty Pants walked straight into a bedroom, looked about and then pulled open a wardrobe door. There was a square shaped box covered with an old sheet in the corner and Farty Pants rapped on the top with his knuckle saying, "There's the telly there man."

He pulled the sheet off and low and behold, there was the very television that had been stolen the night before. The occupant and I were absolutely speechless. Now that was good Police work manufactured from sheer luck!

When I first went into the C. I. D., the office was on the fourth floor and was nearly the length of the building with windows all down one side.

One stormy wet evening, a Detective Sergeant and I were the only ones on duty. I was in the main office working away at my desk, and the Sergeant was through the end in a separate office.

The rain was lashing against the windows and the wind whistling between the gaps of the metal frames, when I heard a noise behind me.

I turned to see the figure of a man wearing a parka coat with the hood pulled over his head walking up the office.

As he neared me, he pulled the hood back, looked around and said, "By, there's a lot of paperwork around here," referring to the piles of files lying on each desk.

I didn't recognize him and jokingly said, "Yes, do you want to take some of it away with you?"

However, he didn't see the funny side. He looked at me with narrowing eyes and said, "What did you say."

I thought 'Oh shit, I've dropped myself in here,' but quietly repeated the question.

The stranger exploded with anger and spat in my face as he bawled, "Do you know who I am clever cunt, I'm only the Detective Superintendent. What's your fucking name clever cunt?"

I said, "D. C. Shepherd sir," and thought, 'I know who you are, I've heard all about you.'

He said, "Right," and stormed off towards the Sergeants office.

As he entered, he frightened the life out of the poor Sergeant as he bawled, "Who the fuck's that clever cunt in there, that D. C. Sharp," and the Sergeant replied, "But we don't have a D. C. Sharp."

"Fuck me, he's given me a false name, come with me," and he swung around and stormed back into the office, by which time I had returned to my paperwork.

As he entered, he pointed to me and shouted, "That's him, what's your name again."

I told him and he turned to the Sergeant and said "Watch him, he's a clever cunt," and stormed off into the night.

That was my introduction to the biggest bastard of a dinosaur the Police ever had, and such a 'clever cunt,' he forgot my name in the space of a minute.

That wasn't the end of the story though.

I knew this particular individual lived not too far from me and some years later after he had retired, I was out jogging on the bridle paths at the bottom end of the estate.

As I made my way along a narrow dirt track covered by overhanging trees, I saw a man walking the same direction in front.

As I neared, I recognised him as the ex-Detective Superintendent.

I continued towards him and as I drew level with his right shoulder, I suddenly quickened my pace, swung my head to the left and bawled, "CLEVER CUNT," into his ear. I ran as quick as ever and did not dare look around to see the expression on his face, although I often wished I had. I bet it was priceless.

I initially worked with a Detective Sergeant who was well known and respected throughout the Force and by the criminal fraternity.

We were investigating a large countrywide cheque fraud and had to travel to just about every major city in England.

At the beginning of the investigation, two Detectives travelled up from London to interview our suspect. They were due to arrive by train at 11.30pm but the Sergeant and I finished at 11pm so we asked the nightshift Detective to meet them and take them for a drink before dropping them off at their hotel, The Five Bridges, which was only 500 yards from Gateshead Police Station.

We should have known better. The nightshift Detective was a guy who was 6ft 6ins tall, as wide as a barn door and who could drink like a whale.

He picked the lads up and took them straight to a local social club.

The following morning, the Sergeant and I started at 9am and we waited until 10am but there was no sign of the London boys.

Eventually we walked over to the hotel and asked the porter to open their room, as we could not get any response from knocking. On entering we found one lying in a pool of sick in the bath, and the other flaked out underneath one of the beds. That added an extra day to their stay.

Some weeks later, the Sergeant and I travelled by train to London to get statements. We stayed two days and before leaving, we contacted the Detective Inspector at Gateshead to tell him we were on our way back. He told us there was a prisoner arrested at a London nick who was wanted at Gateshead for burglary and nonpayment of fines. He said he would arrange for the prisoner to be taken to Kings Cross station to meet us and we could bring him back up with us.

We met the prisoner and escort and I was given his personal property sealed in a bag.

On route back to Newcastle, the prisoner asked what would happen to him.

We told him he would probably serve time for the burglary, and any money he had would probably go towards paying off his outstanding fines.

He asked if he could spend his money as he would rather do the time in prison in lieu of it. The Sergeant agreed and we got the prisoner to endorse my pocket book as receipt for his money.

We then took him to the buffet car.

Five hours later, the train pulled into Newcastle Central Station and we met some uniform Officers who took possession of a very pissed prisoner. One of the Officers commented, "Christ, how pissed was he when you boarded the train?"

The prisoner thought we were the best Policemen he had ever encountered and was a very happy chap indeed.

As part of the same job, another Detective and I travelled to Manchester where the local CID had booked a twin room for us at a large public house/inn.

We booked in during late afternoon, freshened up and then went down to the bar where we ended up in conversation with the Manager.

He told us that he had made a terrible mistake that day. He checked his diary earlier in the morning and thought he saw there was a big party booked that night. He had spent all day preparing food only to be later informed by one of his bar staff that the booking was for the week after. On checking his diary he discovered he had turned two pages over instead of one.

My colleague and I offered our sympathy and enquired if all the food was wasted.

"Well, some of it will go back into the freezer but most will have to be thrown out," he replied and then added, "Would you like some sandwiches?"

Not ones to turn down a good offer, we accepted and he later returned with two plates of corned beef sandwiches.

The next morning we booked out and saw on the bills the tight fisted bastard had added 'SANDWICHES - £1.60p!'

The big detective I mentioned earlier was another animal and as I said, he could drink like a whale and eat like a horse.

I worked with him one Saturday morning and we had to visit an old alcoholic guy who had reported he had been robbed the night before on his way home from the pub.

The big Detective and I went to his house and were invited in.

The room looked and smelt dirty, and there was a table covered in old linoleum in the centre.

A half-finished fish and chip package continually patrolled by a couple of bluebottle flies had been left on the table and as we sat around the table talking to the old man, I could see my colleague looking at the package.

In the middle of the conversation, the big Detective said to the old man, "What's the matter with these then," as he fingered open the newspaper revealing a freezing cold fish supper.

The old man said, "I got them last night but couldn't finish them. Have them if you want," whereupon the big Detective's face lit up and he said, "Cheers mate, I will," as he grabbed the package and stuffed the cold fish and chips into his mouth with his fingers. It was at that point I knew exactly how the queasy cleaner from the earlier story felt.

I got to know a particular Solicitor very well. Our paths crossed frequently during my thirty years in the job. He had his offices not far from Gateshead Police Station and was frequently used by criminals to represent them.

He attended the Police station on one occasion after I had arrested one of his clients for stealing from motor vehicles.

The Solicitor was present when I was interviewing his client who was admitting to quite a few thefts.

I was asking the thief for details of the vehicles he had stolen from as the Solicitor was hunched over his notepad taking details.

While rattling off a list of his crimes, the thief said, "I broke into a blue Ford Orion two weeks ago at the leisure centre."

The Solicitor slowly looked up and said, "What did you steal?"

The thief replied, "I think it was a black sports bags," and the Solicitor shook his head, looked back down at his notes and mumbled, "Yeah, it was my bloody car!"

One of the Detective Sergeants worked from Birtley office and one afternoon, an elderly lady had her bag snatched in the area and the suspect had made good his escape across a local golf course.

As daylight was diminishing, the Detective Sergeant and his Detective Constable made a search of the golf course for any discarded property.

They came across a large locked safe, which was down a grassed dip against brand new metal fencing with waste ground on the other side.

The Detective Sergeant thought it was from a crime and arranged for a lorry to attend the next morning from our vehicle workshops.

I was early shift the following day and the Detective Sergeant delegated two of us to attend the golf course with him to assist in the recovery of the safe.

A lorry with a Land Rover on its back attended as arranged and we obtained permission for the lorry to cross the fairway to the top of the dip.

The lorry had a 'drop back' and winch fitted. The driver unloaded the Land Rover in the car park and drove over to the location of the safe. He backed the vehicle up to the top of the embankment, and fed the winch wire down. We then rolled the safe over onto the wire but noticed someone had chalked 'SCRAP' on the underneath. The Detective Sergeant quickly rubbed the words off thinking that Gateshead C. I. D. would be charged a fee for the attendance of the lorry. It may still have been stolen and we needed to examine it to find out what it contained. The safe was then winched onto the back of the lorry, no problem.

However, when the lorry tried to pull away, the wheels just spun on the wet turf. The lorry just would not move.

The driver then had an idea. He went over to the clubhouse, drove the Land Rover over and attached it to the front of the lorry. We then tried to pull the lorry but the Land Rover wheels spun on the wet turf.

"I've got the wrong tyres on, I'll arrange for the other Land Rover with the winter tyres fitted to attend," said the civilian driver.

About an hour later, the other Land Rover arrived and they attached that to the front of the lorry. Using both Land Rovers, they attempted to pull the lorry away, but due to the weight on its back and the slippery surface, the lorry and two Land Rovers went straight down the embankment, knocking down forty feet of brand new fencing.

The Detective Inspector kept contacting me at the scene asking for updates and on one occasion I jokingly told him we had ordered a helicopter from Bulmer, but the poor stressed out guy didn't see the funny side and just said, "That's not fucking funny Shepherd!"

Eventually, they had to order a heavy recovery lorry from a local firm, which pulled the Police wagon over the waste ground damaging underneath.
We received bills for the repair of our lorry, the hire of the other lorry, and damage to the fencing and fairway, all for a scrap safe.

Everybody suffered embarrassing moments in their career and two in particular always stuck in my mind and make me cringe now just thinking about them. (Well, besides the time I turned up for an early shift wearing a brown shoe on one foot and a black shoe on the other – well it was dark when I got ready and I didn't want to put the light on and wake the wife up. She's never been an early morning good mood person.)
Both happened when I was a Detective and the first was when I attended an elderly couple's house to investigate a burglary.
The lady of the house kindly offered me a cup of coffee which she made with fresh cream. I sat holding the cup and saucer in my hand listening for five minutes to the couple's account of what had happened. I took a sip of coffee and continued to listen. It was at this stage I became aware that the husband was not looking at me as he spoke. I just thought he was one of those people who don't look at you eye to eye, but tend to look over the top of your head as they talk. As his account ended I started to speak and was aware of something wet hitting my chin. I had a five centimetre length of skin from the top of the coffee dangling from my bottom lip!

The second face reddening experience was when another Detective and I attended a company office on the fourth floor of a building. As we were going up in the lift, my colleague said to me, "I've been here before, it's full of dolly birds, here, have a mint to freshen your breath." He must have thought we were going to be greeted with kisses or something.
We both popped a mint sweet into our mouth and entered the office. He was right. There was attractive looking women wearing miniskirts and low cut tops throughout the office, all typing away or answering the telephones.
A guy approached to shake our hands and introduce himself as all the dolly birds watched inquisitively. I thought, 'Well, that was a waste of a mint sweet.'
As I started to speak to him, the mint sweet shot out from my mouth and hit him on the chin then dropped to the floor.

I couldn't apologize enough and finished our business quickly before leaving to smiles and sniggers from an office full of dolly birds.

As we went back down in the lift, the only thing my colleague said while staring at the floor was, "I can't believe you just did that!"

Information was received that a particular Post Office in our area was to be burgled one night and myself and another Detective were delegated to sit inside the premises overnight to await the arrival of the felons.

We went to the premises at about 8pm armed with radios and truncheons, and were locked inside by the key holder who was to return later in the morning to release us.

We hid behind the counter in total darkness and had a good view of the front door and window.

At about 11pm, we saw a man who was obviously heavily intoxicated, approach the large plate glass window. He stopped and put his face close to the glass and started waving. Startled, we looked at each other obviously both thinking, 'how the hell can he see us,' and watched as he stuck his tongue out and pulled stupid faces.

We couldn't believe that anyone, in particular someone inebriated could possibly see us.

We were about to get on the radios to have our colleagues attend to remove him when, after about five minutes of this, he laughed and walked off.

We then realized he had been playing with his own reflection in the window!

One of my partners and I used to socialise a lot immediately after work. We used to go to a floating nightclub on the Gateshead side of the river below the Tyne Bridge.

One night, my colleague, who was on the heavy (if not fat) side, scored with a woman but being so pissed, he couldn't appreciate how ugly she was.

He took her to her house as she gave him directions towards the West End.

She directed him to a house in the roughest part of Newcastle and as they entered the front door in the early hours of the morning, her kids were shouting from upstairs, "Is that you Ma."

My colleague thought, 'well, I'm here now,' and went to bed with her.

However, with him being pissed and her being ugly, he couldn't rise to the occasion.

"You're going to have to do something for me," he suggested.

"What like," she enquired and he replied "Well I don't know, talk dirty to me."

She then said, "Well okay - HOWWAY FATTY, WOP IT UP 'IS!"

For those people who are unaccustomed to the Geordie dialect, that means 'Put your penis into my vagina excessively obese person.'

Unsurprisingly, that didn't work. So as they lay there waiting for something to happen, the woman picked up a toy car that one of her kids had left on the bedside table, and started rolling it back and forward over Fatties bulging stomach. His pecker started to twitch and then stood to attention and he was able to carry out the deed.

The next day he bought a kids toy car and kept it in his bedside drawer.

Whenever he returned home pissed and his wife was feeling frisky, he would get her to roll the toy car back and forward over his belly! (He said a toy dumper truck with six wheels is best).

I got to know a young girl who was a prostitute and she used to give me snippets of information that she had overheard in the pubs on Gateshead High Street.

She was a petite girl with a nice aura about her and a tremendous sense of humour.

She lived on the first floor of maisonette flats at the back of the High Street and to get to her front door, you walked up stairs at one end of the building, and along an open veranda.

I went to see her one night and knocked on the door. She opened it and quickly ushered me in as she looked left and right on the veranda. As she closed the door, I asked what was wrong and she said, "The Vice Squad has set up a camera opposite and are watching everyone who comes and goes."

That was all I needed, subject of a bloody Vice Squad operation.

On returning to the station, I stupidly contacted the Vice Squad and tried to explain why they may have me on film, but the only response I got was, "Ar aye, okay then!"

I had to obtain a statement from my little prostitute and arranged for her to attend Gateshead Police Station. I told one of my colleagues of the arrangements and asked him to be present because, although I got on very well with her, I couldn't trust her one hundred percent.

On the day, we took her to one of the interview rooms where I sat at a table next to her, with her at my right side and my colleague sat at my left and slightly behind.

She was wearing a very short mini skirt, just below the knee boots and a white V necked top.

As I took the statement, I was aware that my colleague was swinging on the back legs of his chair making it blatantly obvious he was bored.

On completion of the statement, the prostitute said to me, "I've got a new tattoo Gordon."

I said, "Have you, that's nice," and she asked, "Do you want to see it."

I was expecting her to roll up a sleeve or something and I said, "Go on then."

She suddenly stood up, pulled up her mini skirt, opened her legs wide, and exposed the fact she had no underwear on at all.

There was a small tattoo of a rose; at least I think it was a rose, on the inside of her thigh.

As she did this, there was an almighty crash behind me as my mate fell backwards on the chair, landing on his back on the floor as the prostitute burst out in hysterics.

I asked if he was okay, because you should always think of your colleague's welfare before you laugh at them, and he stammered, "Fffuckkin' helll."

She was a very naughty girl!

Chapter 4
Newcastle City Centre. Drunks and Shoplifters.

A Police Constable's truncheon. Handy for knocking dents out of Police cars before the Sergeant noticed.

In 1985, I transferred to Newcastle City Centre where I was posted to 'C' relief in uniform, and there I met the patrons of the infamous Bigg Market on my very first night.

The Bigg Market was historically known,and still is renowned as a favourite alcohol drinking area.

Being a youngish lad of tender virtues, I just didn't realize until then how rough some of the females who frequent the City centre were.

I was standing in a shop doorway and saw two girls walking towards me followed by a group of young men. One of the girls was wearing a tiny pair of white 'hot pants' and as they approached me, one of the men behind them, who obviously did not know the girls, ran up and pushed his hand up the leg of her shorts. The girl swung on him and immediately said, "Ha ha ha, shit on, I'm on my rags." His friends burst out laughing as the two girls continued towards me. As they noticed me, the same girl smiled my way and said, "That'll teach the cunt."

Just the kind of girl you take home to meet your mother!

Another night I was sitting alone in a Ford Transit van parked up in the Bigg Market with the driver's window open. The radios were silent, I had no one to talk to and I was bored. As I sat watching people walking past the van, I saw a rather mature female dressed 20 years too young come staggering towards me. She had a bent cigarette clenched between her fingers held at shoulder height, and a crooked smile on her face. With half closed eyes she drunkenly leant her arm against the window frame of my door, looked straight into my eyes and said, "See yee, you've got me creamin' me knickers," and then walked off.

Lovely!

One lad on the shift was a short fat Policeman who had an eye for freebies. In other words he was a right little greedy bastard. I think his motto was 'Owt for nowt'.

One thing an Officer didn't do in those days was walk into a premise, which was not an established tea spot, and just expects a cup of tea for nothing.

I was doubled up with the short fat greedy Policeman one late shift just after moving to Newcastle, and right at the start of our days patrol, he asked if I fancied a cup of coffee. I agreed thinking I was going to find out one of his tea spots, and he drove to a street where there was a large Chinese restaurant. We entered wearing our full Police uniforms and I saw the few couples sitting having meals stop eating and look up at us.

We sat down at a table and a waiter approached with a puzzling look on his face and asked if he could help us.

My colleague said, "Yes, two cups of coffee please."

As we sat waiting, I noticed the waiters and diners continue to look at us and I was suddenly struck with a dreadful thought and said to my colleague, "Have you been here before then," and he replied, "No, it's quite nice isn't it."

After a hasty embarrassing coffee, I paid our dues and never again did I go to a 'tea spot' with the short fat greedy Policeman.

I got to know a local businessman who owned a fish and chip takeaway and restaurant in the Bigg Market, and became very friendly with him. He was from one of the Arab States and was very pro Police. I could call into his place any time and was offered a meal and a cuppa.

Somehow, the short fat greedy Policeman found out about this and one night, he was on foot patrol alone in that area and decided to call in. He stood at the fish and chip counter and asked one of the girls for a packet of chips. She wrapped up the chips in paper then turned and looked at the owner. He gave her a hand signal and she turned back to the short fat greedy Policeman and said, "It's okay, there's no charge."

He then said, "Ah well, can you stick a fish and a fish cake in as well, ta!"

Besides greedy sods, there was always a lazy sod or two on every shift as I mentioned earlier. Some were accepted because they were such likeable people and great characters who added to the shift humour, but others weren't particularly liked because they did nothing and were 'carried' by the rest of the shift.

I was called to investigate a report of a prowler at an art college near the outskirts of the City centre one Friday night when the rest of the shift were battling drunks down the Bigg Market.

I parked the Police car up and walked down an alley between the college buildings, and as I proceeded, I got a feeling that someone was in a door recess ahead of me. I crept down silently and saw one of my shift colleagues in full uniform, with his helmet on the ground and wearing headphones over his ears, doing a Michael Jackson moon dance around his hat.

He jumped out of his skin when I shouted at him and he scurried off as I lambasted him for being a lazy sod and hiding away while his colleagues were fighting drunks.

The same Officer had an unfortunate stutter which seemed to get worse when he was under stress. I was in the custody office one day when this Officer brought a prisoner in who he had arrested for street trading. Street trading or selling items openly without a licence was illegal in Newcastle City centre.

He presented the prisoner before the Sergeant who asked, "What's he arrested for?"

The Officer said, "IIIII've arrested him ffffffor ssssstreet tttttrading Sarge."

The Sergeant turned to the prisoner and asked, "What's your name," and the prisoner said, "JJJJJJimmy."

His stutter was just as bad as my colleagues and I thought, "Christ, that's going to be one hell of a long interview!"

We received an assistance call one night from a British Rail cop at Neville Street outside Newcastle Central Station. On attending, we saw a group of about six or seven skinheads attacking him in a doorway. We waded in and started battling with the skinheads. I arrested one who was only about 5ft 4ins tall, (never fight someone bigger than you), and who was dressed in the typical skinhead uniform of shortened jeans held up with braces, big bovver boots, checked shirt and shaven head. The prisoners were all piled into the back of a Ford Transit van and my skinhead continued to fight all the way back to the station. Even as the van entered the rear yard, the skinhead I hadhold of was kicking, punching and spitting in my face. My father always told me that if I got into a fight, punch the other person's nose. It causes their eyes to water and they can't see. I think I was about 23 years old when he told me that.

So, I thought, 'there's only one way to stop this,' and I punched the skinhead full on the nose. It worked! The skinhead immediately stopped and put its hands to its bloodied nose. At the same time, I saw a female skinhead being led up the steps to the Bridewell cell block, and she pointed to me and shouted, "I don't think he realizes that's a female!"

I thought, 'SHIT!' and then she shouted, "---- and she's three months pregnant!"

'SHIT! SHIT! SHIT!'

A friend of mine I knew before I joined the Police joined the British Transport Police and did his initial training at Dishforth Police Training Centre the same time as I.

The British Transport Police cover the British Rail network and property. He was based at Newcastle Central Railway Station and we would often bump into each other when our shifts coincided.

I was talking to him one Sunday in the portico of the Central Station when I saw a man emerging from the platform area. What caught my eye was the fact that theman's face was blackened and spotted with dead flies, and he had two big white circles around his eyes. I pointed him out to my colleague and he said, "Yeh, he'll be one of the train spotters. They hire old fashioned steam trains to take them on journeys. They don't go anywhere in particular. It's just for the ride. The hard core spotters wear leather World War two flying helmets with goggles and stick their heads out the windows the whole trip to sniff the steam!"

We often received complaints from bus drivers about bus spotters, again usually on Sundays. The spotters were easily identifiable by the three or four cameras slung around their necks and the hundreds of small enameled badges on their hats and jackets.

The spotters would stand on roundabouts or traffic islands and jump out in front of buses to take pictures or obtain fleet numbers. It must have been a bit frightening for the unsuspecting bus drivers to have an idiot jumping out in front as you're hurtling along at 30 mile per hour.

Each bus had its own unique fleet number and the spotters would refer to a bus by that number, much like a person would refer to a boat by its name.

I could just imagine their conversations over a pint;

"You wouldn't believe it but the driver of 1432 spoke to me today. I wrote it in my notebook because it'll probably never ever happen again in my life time."

"Good God man, what did he say?"

"He said, 'Piss off you idiot, you're in my way."

"Fantastic! Can I buy your notebook off you?"

"NO!"

Two Sergeants from my shift were on foot patrol together walking past a well-known public house, a den of iniquity, a house of ill repute, I'm sure you get the picture. As they were passing, an ambulance with blue flashing lights pulled up outside the premises.

As the ambulance men jumped out of the vehicle, one of the Sergeants asked, "What's going on?"

The ambulance man said, "There's a woman inside with a throat obstruction."

The Sergeant said, "She'll be in the men's toilets then!"

Big A. was a giant of a man. He was 6ft 2ins tall and 6ft 1in wide. He must have weighed about 30 stone. He used to buy the largest Y front underpants, snap the elastic and tie string
around them so they would fit his gargantuan waist.

Big A. loved his food and on a late shift, he would go to a fish and chip shop, eat double fish and chips, then return to the station and eat his refreshments he prepared himself, then after work, return home where his mother would have a leek pudding for his supper.

He was a lovely guy and a gentleman. However, he was also handy to have around when trouble was brewing and had a fighting technique called 'The Big A. Splash'.

He basically used his weight to pin violent drunks up against walls or would simply fall on them subduing them on the ground. Big A. wasn't daft. This was the best method to contain drunks and use the least energy to do so.

One refreshment time, four lads on the shift had each purchased fish and chips but just as they were about to sit down, an assistance call came over the radio. They all dashed out dumping the fish and chips on the table.

Big mistake, Big A. was in the same room and being the size he was he couldn't accompany them in such a dash.

Yes, on their return, they found Big A. had eaten the lot! His excuse was he thought they would get cold and didn't want to waste them.

Night shift was a bugger to work. Not the shift itself but the fact it was so hard to get some sleep during the day especially as you got older and especially during the summer months when you had lawn mowers churning away, kids shouting and screaming, dogs barking, etc.

One guy on my shift used to get a mobile butchers van stopping outside his door and tooting on the horn to attract his usual customers.

It wasn't just a single toot; it was a toot toot toot tooooot twice a week.

It was always about two hours after he had finished work and just as he was going into a deep slumber - toot toot toot tooooot!

My colleague wasn't even a customer and having been woken up several times over a matter of months, he waited up one morning and spoke to the butcher.

He explained he worked nightshift and asked the butcher if he could park his van further up the street away from his door.

The butcher was having none of it saying that he would lose his customers if he didn't park up in the same place.

The next time my colleague was on nightshift, he acquired the butcher's home telephone number, waited until 3 o'clock in the morning then rang him.

When the butcher answered the phone, my colleague identified himself as Mister (his name) of (his address) and asked that the butcher drop off a pound of sausage next time he was in his street.

There was a silent pause on the phone and then the butcher said, "Okay mate, I've got the message."

Problem solved!

There was a lad on the shift that I called the Inspector Clouseau of Newcastle, as he was a walking disaster.

He would sometimes park up the Police van and walk away from it having forgot to apply the handbrake, and the van would roll a few yards before someone could stop it.

Or, he could be stopped at red traffic lights while talking to his partner and then suddenly start to drive through them for no apparent reason. Then, on realizing his mistake, he would switch on the blue lights and drive off at high speed to pretend he was going to an emergency.

After duty, he used to go to a local drinking spot where he knew the owner very well.

The owner had refurbishment carried out upstairs to make it into a restaurant and one night, Inspector Clouseau, who was as drunk as a skunk, invited a lady friend upstairs to inspect the new work. The new restaurant was still in the process of being completed and hadn't actually opened to the public.

She was as drunk as him and once out of view of the other patrons; they were in the throes of passion.

He put his hand down her panties and while fumbling around, he found a piece of string.

Being undaunted by this, he pulled it out and threw the attachment under a table and then carried out the dirty deed.

The next morning, the owner had the local Environmental Health Department visiting to authorize the forthcoming opening of the restaurant, and they spotted the 'white mouse' under the table and wouldn't let the new restaurant open for another month.

Some months after, we got a new shift Inspector. He was a great boss who had the facial looks of a boxer and a cleft lip. We had a shift 'do' at a local pub on our days off when I got pissed and the others were egging me on to tell the Inspector what I thought of him. I drunkenly approached him and let fly with "You split lipped bastard; you're the biggest twat I've ever known." He just looked at me and said, "Am I?"

I think I did this just out of drunken idiot behaviour because actually, he was one of the best bosses I ever worked for.

A week later we were on nightshift on the coldest night for years. Everything was covered in white frost. Very early in the morning, the Inspector told another lad and I to change into civilian clothing as information had just been received that a military museum at Exhibition Park on the outskirts of the City was going to get burgled. The information was that the burglars were approaching the building from over fields at the back and we had to keep observations for them.

We got changed and equipped with radios and torches and got dropped off on the perimeter of the park. We walked over to the building and stood, unsheltered in the freezing cold for three hours.

At two minutes to finishing time, the radio controller called us, "From the Inspector, return to the station, and can you break the ice for the ducks before you come back."

That was his revenge, but not the end of the story. A girl on the shift was very well endowed in the chest region. She worked in the control room at the City centre Police Station and one day a few of the lads were talking while driving around. One of them was Big A. and as he began to speak, someone pressed down the transmit button on a radio and the well-endowed Policewoman got a clear transmission of, "Hey, that was great when Gordon Shepherd told the Inspector what he thought of him the other night, did you hear what he said, and what do you think about the size of (the Police Woman's) tits!"

Princess Margaret, the Queens sister, was visiting the Newcastle Civic Centre one night for a function of some sort. A Sergeant and I were delegated to man the main entrance to await her arrival.

The entrance overlooked a small park directly in front and as we saw the Royal cars entering the Civic Centre about 200 yards from where we were standing, I happened to look towards the park and saw a female tramp walking through about 50 yards from us.

I said to the Sergeant, "Look at her," as the cortege neared.

As we looked towards her, the tramp suddenly yanked up her clothing, pulled her grimy knickers down and proceeded to take a dump right in front of us.

The Sergeant's eyes nearly popped out his head and he ran towards her shouting, "You dirty cow, piss off," chasing her from the Princesses view and just in time as the cars pulled up at the main entrance.

As she got out of the car, Princess Margaret thanked a rather flustered Sergeant for securing her arrival. She had no idea how close it was!

I was probably the only Police Officer in the Force, if not the country, who could say, 'I groped a Judges arse!'

The same Sergeant that saved Princess Margaret's sight called me back to the station one morning and explained that a female Judge on route to the Crown Court had broken down outside the Police station and I was required to transport her directly to the Crown Courts which were situated a few miles to the north of the City centre.

Now this Crown Court Judge carried a bit of a reputation and was feared by everyone who appeared before her, including Police Officers and barristers.

I tried to explain that I was driving a Ford Transit van and it wasn't really suitable for a five foot tall portly built female Judge but the Sergeant was having none of it.

"Just get her to the Courts as soon as possible, she's late!"

I escorted the Judge to the passenger side of the van and opened the door. As she heaved herself up into the passenger seat she started to fall back and I instinctively put my hands up and onto each rounded buttock. As I pushed her up, it flashed through my mind, 'Oh my God, I've just indecently assaulted a Crown Court Judge, and it had to be the most feared Judge of them all.'

However, as she positioned herself in the seat, her head slowly turned and with a twinkle in her eye and a very slight grin, she said, "Well, thank you Officer."

Not a lot was said on route but some months later, I was at the Crown Courts as a witness and this particular Judge was presiding. As I stood in the witness box and introduced myself, she looked across at me and with a Mona Lisa type smile, she said, "Ah yes, the Officer who kindly gave me a lift - in more ways than one!"

Another claim to fame as far as famous people are concerned is that I caused the football manager Brian Clough to be quiet during a game of football. It was no easy task as he had a hell of a reputation for shouting and swearing at people.

Newcastle United was managed by Willie McFaul and Brian Clough was manager of Nottingham Forest. They were playing against each other one Saturday and I was standing between the two manager's dugouts at the side of the pitch.

I hated working the football matches. I never had any interest in the game and although I was doing it for overtime, it was always bloody hard work. I learned very quickly to always wear a plastic coat because they were much easier to wipe the spit off, but useless at keeping the cold out.

During the game, Brian kept jumping up, running over to Willie McFaul and angrily shouting obscenities. Then he would return to his dugout, but two minutes later he was up again lambasting poor Willie.

Swearing then wasn't as accepted as it is today and of course every time Brian jumped up the fans were getting excited.

After about five or six times, I'd had enough and the next time he jumped up I stepped in front of him, pointed a finger and said, "You, sit down and pack in the swearing."

He looked at me and said, "Why, are you going to arrest me or something," and I said, "Not only arrest you, but march you straight across the middle of the pitch in front of forty thousand fans, now sit the fuck down!"

His backside hit the bench and he didn't move until the final whistle blew!

The Magistrates Court building was attached to the Police station and when you worked in the City, you were sometimes required to work Court duties.

Basically, you were showing a uniform presence to prevent any trouble and assist in escorting prisoners from the cells to the courtroom.

Two memorable incidents when I was performing these duties were firstly when a Police Officer of tender years was giving evidence regarding a man he had arrested for being drunk and disorderly.

The Officer was obviously nervous and when he was asked what the drunk had called him, he replied, "He called me a Magistrate your bastard!"

The other was when a well-known drug addict who frequented the City was appearing before the Court for possession of heroin.

As he stood in the dock, the Magistrates informed him they were considering a custodial sentence, whereupon the druggy pulled a box of Swan Vesta matches from his pocket, slid the box open and held it to his mouth saying, "Beam me up Mr. Spock, I'm in trouble!"

I was working night shift and in the early hours of the morning an excited hurried voice from one of my colleagues boomed over the radio, "I'm on the walkway above Newbridge Street looking over towards the east and I can see a large fire. Whatever it is, it's really got a hold and it's like Towering Inferno."

The control room then contacted me asking if I could drive down to the Quayside to see if I could find its exact location.

I knew exactly what it was but gave it a few minutes before getting back on the radio to control saying, "I've spoken to a man at Monkton coke works who says he's looking towards Newcastle where he can see something that looks like a Policeman on a walkway looking at his fire!"

One late shift, I was doubled up with a male probationer when we found a window broken at the back of a shop.

I said to the probationer, "You go around the front and I'll climb in through this window and I'll let you in the front door so we can search the premises."

So off the probationer went as I climbed in through the broken window and then made my way through to the front of the premises. I opened the main door but the probationer was nowhere to be seen. I stepped out the doorway looking left and right and saw the probationer standing two doors down, so I shouted to him. I watched in disbelief as he bent down at the door where he was standing, put his lips to the letter box and shouted, "I can hear you but I can't see you."

The probationers always provided the best laughs!

A guy on the shift had a particular party trick which he used frequently on weekend nights down the Bigg Market. He would walk up to scantily dressed young women , sniff their necks while peering down their low cut tops, and try to identify their perfume. His success rate was about eight out of ten so he obviously did this trick a lot and had learnt to identify most of the perfumes.

I was standing with him one hot sunny afternoon in Northumberland Street when he spotted a pretty and very smart female walking towards us. She had a brooch on her lapel with the letter 'D' and a red design around it. My partner took one step in front of her and said, "That's a nice brooch you've got, let me guess, Dianne?"

She said, "No."

"Well, you look like a Dawn?"

"No."

"Is it Doris?"

"No."

"Alright, you've got me, what are you?"

"DIABETIC!"

There was a Sergeant on the shift everyone referred to as 'thrombosis' because he was considered to be like a slow moving clot.

We had a new microwave oven installed at Pilgrim Street Police station and not many people had used one, including the Sergeant.

One day he brought a mince pie in for his refreshments and asked someone how long he should put it in the microwave. They jokingly told him fifteen minutes, not expecting him to fall for it, but he did.

The station was clouded with thick stinking smoke and his pie looked exactly like an Oxo cube.

The fire alarms activated and the Fire Service from next door drove two fire engines fifty yards with sirens blaring and lights flashing to check everything was okay.

It was a bit embarrassing for the Sergeant explaining his mince pie was to blame.

I was on my own one night driving the panda car in the Bigg Market when I saw this drunken giant of a man holding a 16" pizza box in one hand and sticking two fingers up towards me with the other while mouthing, "Yer black twat, come on, let's have ya."

He was built like the back end of a double decked bus, just as wide and just as tall, and had fists like railroad hammers.

There weren't many of us on the shift at that particular time and everyone else was busy with other jobs or paperwork. I looked at this guy and thought, 'Christ, he's going to kill me.'

I stopped the car, got out and shouted over from a distance, "Why don't you just eat your pizza and go home." He shouted back in the deepest booming voice, "What the fuck are you going to do like?" I thought, 'Here we go,' and said, "Lock you up."

He said, "Right," and came towards me. As I prepared myself for the mother of all Bigg Market battles, he pulled open the back door of the Police car, pushed his bulk in while still holding his pizza and said, "Right, you've locked me up." He took up the whole of the back seat and as the car tilted slightly backwards with his weight, I drove back to the station as fast as I could before the tyres burst, while my prisoner munched away at his supper. It was just as well the car had rear wheel drive otherwise we would never have moved.

On arrival, he squeezed out and I lead him into the Bridewell, the cell block at Pilgrim Street Police Station where the Sergeant asked what he was arrested for.

Now up to this point, I had probably been perceived by the Bridewell staff as some sort of hero. A 5ft 9in Policeman (in his platform Doc Martens) locking up a Bigg Market monster on his own.

However, before I could answer, matey said, "Drunk and disorderly Sarge, I've been a naughty lad, I called the Officer some horrible things and deserve what's coming."

Bang went the hero status!

I seem to remember he received a caution the next morning, which I was pleased about because I doubt if the Magistrates would have believed my account!

Some people made the job far too easy. It was unbelievable how many drunken people mistaken Police cars for taxis and attempt to flag you down to take them home.

I was wearing full Police uniform parked up one night in a marked police car when a lad, who was obviously drunk on alcohol and high on drugs, pulled open the passenger door, got in and said to me, "I've got no money mate but I'll give you some snort (cocaine) if you take me home," and produced three small plastic bags of white powder from his trouser pocket.

Pleasantly shocked, I said to him, "You do know this is a Police car don't you," but he laughed and said, "Yeh, right, good one mate." I said, "No, it really is and you're locked up." He looked at me and there was a pause as his pea sized brain took in the information and then he said, "Fuck!"

Why do drunken males always think they are the best fighters in the world? Due to their alcoholic consumption they have little balance, little stamina and no coordination at all.

A young male who had been involved in a fight approached me one Friday night in the Bigg Market and I noticed his jaw was over to the left side of his face. I thought to myself, 'That's not right', as he pointed to the dislocation and said to me, "Can you punch it back into place." I said, "No I can't, you need to go to hospital mate." He replied, "I can't do that, it means less drinking time," and walked off. Unbelievable!

There was a small group of us who more or less arrived on the shift about the same time.

One lad had transferred from the Shoplifting Squad. He hated everyone, even himself, and was another ram. Women fell over themselves to get serviced by this stag.

We hated going nightclubbing with him because as soon as we walked in, he would spot someone and say, "Number two reserves in," and that was usually the last we saw of him that night.

The Stag was always angry about something and frequently used the 'F' word. I used to call him 'a horrible little man' because that's exactly what he was, but in a comical kind of way.

We were teamed up one nightshift in a van when, at about 3am, we received a call to the effect a couple of drunks were walking down Dene Street towards the Quayside kicking shop windows as they went. We attended but could not see anyone in the vicinity. The Stag suggested we drove down to the Quayside and as we did so, we saw two young men just about to walk over the Swing Bridge towards Gateshead.

The Stag started to move excitedly in his seat as he said, "There's the fuckers, pull them up."

As I pulled alongside them, The Stag jumped out and approached them and the conversation went as follows -

"What the fuck do you twats think you're playing at?""I'm sorry Officer."

"You will be fucking sorry if you broke a window won't you."

"I'm sorry Officer; I don't know what you mean."

"Don't fucking give me that, you know what I'm talking about you fucker, now I suggest you fuck off quick before I fucking lock you up. Where the fuck are you going anyway?"

"Well actually, we're returning to Durham University, we're both trainee priests!"

That same week, we were driving down Northumberland Street when a small guy about 5ft 3ins tall with a bloody nose flagged us down.

The Stag's sixth sense came into play (ex-Vice Squad) and he said, "He's a faggot, drive past."

I said, "You can't do that man," and pulled over.

The guy said in a very squeaky effeminate voice, "Officer, Officer, I've just been attacked."

We got the story out of him but he did not want to make any form of complaint. He agreed to us taking him to the local hospital and we dropped him off at the Casualty Department.

As we drove away, The Stag said, "I bet we get another call from there saying he's causing trouble."

No sooner had he spoke, a message came over the radio that someone in the Casualty Department was working themselves. The Stag jumped up and down in his seat in an excited manner and said, "I told you, the fucking puff is causing trouble, get back quick."

We attended and The Stag ran into the Casualty, spotted the guy sitting in the waiting area, grabbed him by the shoulders from behind and lifted him out of his seat. As he carried the man out with his feet waggling in thin air, a nurse ran up and said, "It's not him Officer, it's the other man over there," pointing to a drunk on the other side of the department.

The Stag dropped the guy to his feet and the guy said, "I want an apology Officer."

The Stag looked at me and thinking it may stop any complaints from being made, I said, "You better apologize."

In a barely audible voice, he whispered, "I'm sorry," and the little man said, "I can't hear you." The Stag repeated in a slightly louder voice, "I'm sorry," but again the guy said, "I still can't hear you."

I'm fairly sure that the guy was winding The Stag up but unfortunately, he did not know the boundary of The Stag's temper. The Stag shouted across the whole Casualty department, "I'M FUCKING SORRY YOU FUCKING FAGGOT!"

The Stag and I once caught two men engaging in sexual activities with each other. While out on foot patrol we heard a noise, looked over a wall and saw one guy on his knees in front of another performing oral sex.

We arrested them and the matter later went to the Magistrates Court where we were required to attend to give evidence.

I gave my account and then sat in the Court as The Stag entered and stood in the witness box.

In his evidence he said that the guy receiving the oral sex had a look of ecstasy on his face. When it came to the turn of the defence Solicitor to fire the questions, the first thing he asked The Stag was, "What exactly is a look of ecstasy."

The Stag looked uncomfortable as he spluttered, "Well, he looked as though he was enjoying himself."

The defence Solicitor, who was obviously enjoying this as much said, "Yes, but what exactly is a look of ecstasy, can you show us Officer?"

I couldn't believe it as I watched The Stags face contorted into what he thought was a look of ecstasy. He stood with this strained stupid grin on his face and his head tilted to one side. It looked more like bloody pain to me!

We won the case but I couldn't wait to get back to the station to tell everyone about the Stags painful look of ecstasy.

Another good friend on the shift was at least twenty stone in weight, and carried a big sense of humour.

He was sitting on the toilet one morning and an Officer, who was from another shift, was in the cubicle next to him.

This other Officer was the most horrible dirty man I have ever known. He was ex-military and had learned every trick in the book before joining the Police.

He used to take great pride in pulling snots from his nose, holding them up in front of you and challenging you to make bigger ones. I once saw him pull a green snot from his nostril and when it was still attached, stretch it at least seven centimetres from his nose. Suddenly, it slipped from between his fingers and pinged back up his nose nearly giving him whiplash in the process.

Getting back to the story, the cubicles were separated by wooden screens with gaps at the bottom and top. As my overweight colleague sat contemplating the world, a newspaper bearing a false doggy turd slowly slid under the partition towards him from the other side. It was the kind of realistic plastic turds you can buy in joke shops.

However, my colleague didn't know this and being aware of who was next door, my colleague shouted, "You dirty little bastard," as the newspaper was quickly yanked back disappearing from view.

My colleague sat nervously looking about as, unknown to him; the other Officer rolled up a piece of paper into a ball and threw it over the top. As my colleague saw it coming, he screamed, thinking it was the turd and fell off the toilet jamming himself between the pot and the wall, with his trousers and underpants still around his ankles. It took three of us to pull him out from his predicament and it wasn't a pretty sight!

A regular tea spot on night shift was a local hotel which was manned during the night by three porters who were only too pleased for us to pop in and relieve their boredom. So, in the early hours if it was quiet, a group of us would raid the large fridge of cream cakes, downed with fresh coffee, and then relax in the big leather Chesterfield sofas in reception which were so comfortable after plodding the streets for hours, it was hard not to fall asleep.

On our arrival one night we found the porters sitting around a young lad who was obviously drunk but wide awake, and an older chap who was obviously drunk and out for the count. A coffee table in front of the pair was fully laden with empty drinks glasses, some of which were stacked precariously.

The young lad was very excited at our presence and explained a group of about twenty men who called themselves the Edinburgh Social Club, but who hailed from Liverpool, annually travelled to Newcastle to stay for a drunken weekend. This was his first visit with the club and had made a bet with the others he would be the 'last man standing.' He wanted us to witness his success.

As we spoke, the older man slowly arose from the seat in his sleep and without opening his eyes, pulled down his fly, took out his flaccid penis and commenced urinating over the coffee table. A porter grabbed one of the empty glasses and positioned it to catch the outpour. The man filled two glasses with one and a half pints of amber piss then put himself away, sat down and resumed his peaceful slumber.

This was the icing on the cake for the young lad and he begged us to return the following night to inform the club members of the event. However, we thought better of it.

A few years later, I walked into the front reception area of Pilgrim Street Police Station and saw the same young lad at the counter.

I greeted him and reminded him of the above incident to identify myself, then asked what he was doing. He told me he had returned to Newcastle with the club for their annual outing, and had picked up a couple of girls in the Bigg Market with his friend. After between one to fifteen pints they invited the girls back to their hotel room. One couple ended up on the bed and the other in the bathroom.

Having attempted drunken sexual activities, both the lads fell asleep.

When they awoke a few hours later, the girls had disappeared with £300 of the lad's spending money.

I don't think he was impressed when I remarked it must have been the most expensive shag he'd ever had in his life.

I had a refresher driving course at Police Headquarters and on my arrival; the administration department claimed they had not received my accommodation request. Due to shortage of available rooms, they put me on an empty floor, with females on the floor below and males on the floor above. For some unbelievable reason, the bosses thought an empty floor between the two sexes kept them apart.

Anyway, on the first night, I was lying in bed and could hear bedsprings pinging in a consistent rhythm, male and female grunts and groans, and a record playing over and over again from the room below. Each time the record ended, the pinging bedsprings stopped, someone got out of bed, put the same record back on, then made bedspring accompaniment again.

It went on for ages and even though I was tired and annoyed at being unable to sleep, I was also impressed by their stamina and constant rhythm.

The following night, I was in the campus social club and was chatting to a lad I knew from Gateshead who was on a dog handlers course. I said to him, "Last night I never slept a wink because some bastard was shagging downstairs all night. They kept playing this fucking record over and over again, I couldn't believe it."

He looked at me with an expression of deep thought then after a few seconds said, "It wasn't 'Rumours' by Fleetwood Mac by any chance was it," and I said, "Yes it was."

He then said, "Hey I'm sorry about that, it's the only record she brought!"

There was a ginger haired guy on the same course who I knew from my Gateshead days and one day, he was driving the training car in the Blyth area on the North East coast line.

The instructor was in the front passenger seat and I was in the rear.

We approached a railway crossing and the instructor pointed and said to Ginger, "What would you do if the car broke down while crossing the tracks."

Ginger pondered for a moment and then said, "You see those houses next to the crossing," pointing to a small group of terraced houses.

The instructor looked and said, "Yes."

Ginger said, "I would knock on all the doors and say come out here because you are about to see the biggest fucking smash you'll ever see!"

I was out on mobile patrol one early shift when, just as traffic volume was at its peak, I received a report of a non-injury road traffic accident on the Tyne Bridge.

On attending, I saw a Volvo estate had run into the back of a skip lorry. The sight was horrendous. There was blood and bits of gory body lying all over the front bonnet of the Volvo and on the road between the two vehicles. Even I got a fright on seeing the mess wondering what the hell had happened, but I soon established that the skip was full of animal offal that had spilt over the top on impact.

Accidents always attracted the passing drivers who slow down to two miles per hour and crane their necks to have a look. They cause massive traffic backups for which the Police usually get the blame. These people are referred to as 'rubberneckers.'

People passing must have thought the worst of me as I sat for three quarters of an hour waiting for City Council cleansing department to arrive, absolutely pissing my pants with laughter at the look on people's faces as they slowly drove past 'rubbernecking' and then suddenly spotting the gore lying in the road.

I know this is backtracking a bit, but when I worked at Gateshead, I once dealt with an accident on the Gateshead flyover where traffic used to build up to a practical standstill heading towards the Tyne bridge every morning.

A man was driving towards the bridge on the way to a wedding and didn't see the stationary traffic in front. He had a very large three tier strawberry gateaux on the rear seat of his car, which ploughed into the rear of a car in front. As it collided, the back of his driver's seat snapped putting him flat on his back as the car continued hitting another three vehicles before coming to a rest against the roadside barriers.

Luckily, the driver was not seriously injured but as he stepped out of his car, other people were absolutely horrified to see he was covered from head to toe in a red and white dripping gooey mess.

Newcastle City centre had more than its fair share of flying rats, or pigeons as most people call them.

A lot of them for some reason had deformed feet, I presume having caught them on anti-pigeon netting or something, and although I hate killing any living creature, I didn't mind if I accidentally ran over a dirty flying rat occasionally.

Actually, because they were so street wise and traffic wary, it only happened once to me that I am aware of.

It was a sunny hot Saturday afternoon and the City was busy with traffic adding to the static fumes, and pedestrians were weaving down the footpaths like colonies of ants.

I was driving a Police marked Ford Transit van in Clayton Street and didn't even see the pigeon until I heard a very loud bang from the rear offside tyre.

As the wheel of the van had gone over the stupid thing that obviously didn't have the sense to get out of the way, it exploded.

I immediately looked in my drivers mirror and saw the flattened body with a wing sticking up in the air flapping about.

That's when I realized all the pedestrians had stopped and were looking towards me. Kids holding there mummy's hands were rubbing their tearful eyes, people were pointing with wide eyes and mouths agape, and shop assistants came out of the buildings to see what was happening.

I drove on with my head held in shame.

And then laughed my head off as I went around the corner!

I received a call on my radio one late shift that a tenant at a street within the City centre thought there was a burglar in his house. The large houses were built in the 1800's and had three storeys and a basement.

I attended and met the occupant at the front door, a young man of about 22 years of age. He showed me in and whispered he thought he had heard someone creeping around the house but had been too frightened to investigate. I explained that if he followed behind me, I would check each room on each floor starting on the ground floor, then basement, then the upper floors.

As we silently went through each room, I was aware that the occupier stayed very close behind me, too close actually. I went into the first room, saw there was no one there, and turned to check the next room. As I turned, I saw a pistol held by the occupier at head height pointing into my face. I violently swiped the gun to one side grabbing the barrel and shouted, "What the fuck…"

The occupier whispered, "It's just a replica to frighten the burglar."

I said, "Frighten the burglar! I've just nearly shit myself you stupid bastard!"

There wasn't a burglar in the house and the occupier had a seriously burnt lug hole on my departure!

In the very early hours of the morning, we received a report of three burglars entering the rear of a shop in the Gallowgate area. We duly attended and posted an Officer at the front window of the shop, while the others went to the rear and waited for the burglars to emerge from the smashed in door.

As the burglars came out and saw all the Police, one gave himself up, but the other two ran back into the shop pursued by Officers, and through to the front where they were trapped between the pursuers and the plate glass shop window with an Officer on the outside.

Now this particular Officer had a skill in prisoner psychology called 'The Naa Naa technique,' which he then demonstrated.

He placed both his thumbs in each of his ears with his fingers spread apart and palms waving, contorted his face, jumped up and down and shouted, "Naa Naa Na Na Naa."

It was reported that the two prisoners who witnessed this later said to the Sergeant at the Police Station, "If we tell you everything, will you make sure that Policemen gets treatment!"

A lad who became and remains a good friend of mine was a hell of a character. He lived out in the country near Hexham and besides being a falconer; he kept a variety of animals including cattle, sheep, geese, snakes, ferrets, chipmunks, chickens and sometimes pigs.

He was also into fishing, horse riding and SCUBA diving.

On nightshift, he used to bring a European Eagle Owl with a six feet wingspan into work. It used to stand on the backrest of a sofa when we played cards during our break time, and used to look over our shoulders at the cards. The only time it hooted was when someone had a good hand, and strangely, Country Boy would always win that game.

Country Boy and three others were going fishing one rest day and travelled to their destination in a small van with closed sides. Country Boy and his mate, who was another giant of a man, were in the seat-less back, and the other two were in the front.

After a while, Country Boy became bored and decided to liven up the atmosphere up by jokingly saying to the driver, "I think you better pull over, I need a crap."

Thinking that Country Boy was being serious the driver replied, "We're nearly there, hang on."

After about ten minutes, Country Boy again said, "Look, you better pull over, I'm starting to get desperate," and again the driver told him to hang on. By this time his mate who was in the back with him had a worried look on his face and kept nervously looking at Country Boy.

After another ten minutes, Country Boy said, "I'm telling you, I can't wait any longer, the old brown trout is starting to show his head."

Once again he was told to hang on as they were nearly there but Country Boy suddenly blurted, "Right, that's it, I'm having a shite," and started to unloosen his trouser belt and drop his trousers.

The 6ft 6ins long body of his mate dived over to the front between the driver and passenger, forcing the driver to an emergency stop in a lay-by as Country Boy dropped his pants.

The other three jumped out of the van, ran around to the back and pulled the doors open to be faced by Country Boy bending over with his trousers around his ankles baring his backside, just as a French couple pulled in behind them thinking that the lads were in trouble.

Country Boy took me badger watching at a sett in woods about a mile from his house.

We rigged up an old rotten tree trunk horizontally between two trees seven feet off the ground above the sett.

We climbed up and Country Boy sat at one end and I at the other both hugging the tree trunks for about forty minutes in complete silence and without twitching or moving.

As we sat, I heard an almighty loud squeak as a painfully held in fart finally escaped from the tight clenched cheeks of Country Boy's arse.

I looked over to Country Boy who had a stupid grin on his face just as a couple of badgers appeared below us, sniffed the air, twisted their faces and then disappeared back down the sett and did not show again that night.

As I said earlier, Country Boy kept an unusual assortment of animals and was a bit of a part time farmer, occasionally raising sheep and cattle for slaughter.

He once had a bull slaughtered and brought two massive joints of beef into work for the shifts lunch break. He kept a lovely looking milking cow with big brown eyes and long lashes.

During the winter one year, he was in the paddock spreading a bale of hay around for the cow, which unknown to Country Boy, was feeling rather frisky.

As he was bending over with his back to the cow, a hoof suddenly came over his shoulder and before he could utter, "Bless my cotton socks," (or other expletives nothing like that), a second hoof draped over his other shoulder.

In a micro second, as the weight of the cow was pushing him to the ground, Country Boy realized he was going to be crushed, so he pulled himself forward.

Unfortunately, with him pulling forward, and the weight of the cow pushing down, he was propelled violently straight into the brick wall of his barn, breaking his collarbone.

Apparently, he then picked up a fork and forgetting the pain, he chased the cow all around the paddock screaming blue murder at the poor animal, swiping with the implement held high in one hand, and his other arm dangling limply on the other side.

On our rest days, some of us on the shift used to hire a van and go hiking near Newton Stewart in Scotland. We would spend the day hiking, freshen up at our hotel and have a pub crawl at night, then returned home the following day.

On one occasion, as we dropped Country Boy off at his home, I asked him to get his Burmese python to show the lads. As I said it, one of the lads said, "Snake! Not when I'm here!" and jumped out the side door of the van and ran about a hundred yards down the road.

Country Boy brought a beautiful yellow coloured large snake from his house, showed everyone then returned indoors.

I shouted to the lad standing down the road that we were leaving but he insisted that I drive further on past the house as he feared Country boy would run out with the snake.

I drove off as instructed and the lad sprinted past the house and jumped in the side door shouting, "DRIVE, DRIVE!"

As I drove away, someone sitting behind the petrified lad took a banana from his bag and draped it over the lads shoulder.

I nearly crashed the van as this almighty high pitched scream stabbed my ear drums.

I swear I momentarily went deaf.

For a while after that, the poor snake hater received hissing phone calls and rubber snakes through the internal post, and I put my hands up to being responsible for sending a rubber snake. Vengeance for the racing heart beat and bloody earache I suffered.

Being a country boy, it was inevitable that Country Boy would have been in the Mounted Section or 'The Horsing Around Lot' as we called them, at some time in his career, and at the end, he gave one of the funniest retirement speeches I have heard.

I remember nearly falling off my chair with laughing when referring to his time in the Horse Section he said; "If there's one thing I've learned in this job over the years, it's this. Never, ever, hose out the back of a horse lorry in the middle of a freezing winter, load it up with three horses, drive down a very steep hill and then brake sharply at the bottom!"

Just imagining the scene as he said it had tears in my eyes, although I don't suppose the poor horses were too pleased at the time.

I took a Tutor Constable course at Headquarters which authorised me to train probationers, and on returning to Newcastle City centre I was immediately delegated to look after a probationer who had just come out of the Merchant Navy.

He was a more mature probationer, but it is very difficult as you get on in service to appreciate that new starters are as green as grass and haven't a clue about the job at all, no matter how old they are.

He used to do daft things like issue drivers with the copy of a fixed penalty ticket that he should have kept, and I became dreadful of his deep southern voice saying, "Er Gordon, I think I've made a mistake."

We stopped a car going through a 'NO ENTRY' road traffic sign and I told him to issue the driver with a fixed penalty ticket. As he wrote it out, I was looking about observing life and as the offending vehicle drove off, the probationer said the spine chilling words, "Er Gordon, I've made another mistake."

"Ar man, you haven't give him the copy again have you," I asked, and pointing down the road he said, "No, he's driven off with my hat!"

As I looked, I saw the car stopped at traffic lights further down the road with a Police helmet sitting on the roof. Luckily, it fell off as the car pulled away and the probationer had to run down the road to retrieve it.

We had civilian Matrons employed in the Bridewell to help with the wellbeing of prisoners and search females.

A well-known alcoholic girl frequented the city centre on a regular basis, and had a habit of stripping off to her underwear, or further sometimes, and openly touting on the street for business.

Her speciality was oral sex which she performed to get money for alcohol.

I arrested her one day for being drunk and disorderly and, unusually for her, she had her clothes on. She was wearing a skirt and green coloured singlet vest.

I took her to the Bridewell and as she was being searched by one of the matrons, the matron said to her indicating to her chest just under her chin, "What have you got there on your chest?"

The girl wiped her mouth with the back of her hand saying, "Ar, I've just finished a guy off before I got arrested," at which the matron put her hand to her mouth and ran off to the nearest toilet.

Chapter 5
Plain Clothes

A Police woman's truncheon. Only 26cm long, they said they were only good for one thing. I never found out what that one thing was.

After about a year in uniform at Newcastle, I was posted to the Shoplifting Squad in the City centre and worked with a Detective Sergeant who had an amazing full crop of the most brilliant white hair.

Early one morning, we were in the Shoplifting Squad Office, which was on the first floor. It was a Saturday and everything was still and quiet. The Sergeant was standing beside the window and I was sitting opposite. We were talking and both looking out of the window at this pure white pigeon that was sitting on a window ledge at the same level as us on the opposite side of the street.

As we watched, the pigeon took off from the ledge and in a kind of slow motion movement, glided across the street towards our office directly towards the Sergeant, and splattered spread-eagled up against the glass of our window. It slid down to the ledge, shook its head, then took off again, and I swear to this day that the pigeon had thought that the Sergeant's head was another shaggable pigeon.

I arrested two women who had been shoplifting together. They were fully admitting to what they had done but had never been arrested before and were a bit concerned as to the consequences. On route to the station I assured them everything would be okay and I would look after them.

As the Sergeant was taking their details, another Officer entered the Bridewell with a local well known tramp.

This particular tramp was the dirtiest, smelliest tramp you could imagine and had a thick matted beard.

The Sergeant decided to deal with the tramp first and put the two women in a holding cell within the charge room. The holding cell was basically a small area of the room caged off and containing a bench to sit on. Occupants had a full view of proceedings in the charge room.

The women watched as the tramp was searched and as the searching Officer put his hand into his coat pocket, he brought out an old sodden sandwich dripping with green mouldy mayonnaise which the tramp had obviously found in a bin.

As it emerged from his pocket, the tramp suddenly snatched it from the Officers hand and crammed into his own mouth, dribbling the green mayonnaise through his beard.

The two women were frantically holding their hands to their mouths to stop vomiting as the Officer grabbed the tramps hands to stop him eating more.

After they took him to the cells, I jokingly told the girls there were no more cells left for them and they would have to share with the tramp.

Do you know, I wouldn't be surprised if those girls never got arrested again.

Dealing with shoplifter's everyday was a bit repetitive and to relieve the boredom we had a bit of a competition going on between the lads on the squad involving interviews. Before interviewing a punter, one of your colleagues would give you a keyword you had to get in the tape recorded interview.

I remember two in particular that I had to say. One was 'antelope' and the other was 'Afghanistan.' The first was easy. I said to the punter, "Is it correct that as you were approached by the store detective, you ran off like an antelope being chased by a lion?" With a very quizzical look, he said, "No, I just stood still."

The other was a bit harder but after deep thought during the interview, I came out with the following, "You know, if you had done this in Afghanistan, they would have cut your hands off."

The punter had a look of horror on her face but her Solicitor raised his eyebrows and obviously wasn't impressed at all!

Most of the big stores in the City centre had their own remote control security cameras situated throughout the buildings, which were monitored and controlled from their security offices. The systems all had recording facilities, and were used to back up the store detectives in obtaining evidence and identifying unknown shoplifters.

One day I was asked to attend a large store in the Eldon Square shopping malls where one of the store detectives told me her colleague had recorded two suspected males acting suspiciously inside the store the day before. She asked if I could identify them and commenced playing the video recording. As we watched, her colleague walked into the office and said, "Hi Gordon, did she tell you about those two lads yesterday." As she said it and before I could answer, she looked at the monitor screen and suddenly said, "Christ, they're back in at the same display," and ran out of the office in pursuit of the previous day's video recording.

The Shoplifting Squad office was shared with the Stolen Vehicle Squad, and they used to go out to various car parks in the City to keep observations from static points.
The Cattle Market car park was always a favourite with car thieves and the lads used to observe the area from an office attic window overlooking one side of the car park.
One day, they saw a lone male enter the car park with his hands in his pockets and looking around from side to side, checking cars as he walked past. His body language and their instinct told them this guy was going to do something and they continued to watch as he walked straight through the unattended vehicles looking furtively about. They relayed radio messages to other Officers in the area, to pounce as soon as he did the deed. Everybody was quickly in position with marked cars parked just out of sight and plain clothed Officers hiding behind walls and cars. There was an air of excitement and the adrenaline was flowing as they waited for the call.
However, he went to the far side of the car park where there were no cars, knelt down, looked about, took a book from inside his jacket which he lay open in front of him, took out his erect penis and masturbated furiously!

Sometimes I worked with the Stolen Vehicle Squad if they were short staffed and one afternoon, I was working with a colleague in plain clothes keeping observations on car parks on the outskirts of the City centre.
Up to this point I had never really thought about my general fitness. As a young(ish) man, fitness is just part of being young but you tend to forget as you get older that the body is very slowly stiffening up and muscles are slowly diminishing.
We spotted a young lad trying to break into unattended cars and chased after him. He ran off into a nearby housing estate but from the outset, he and my colleague had left me at the starting line and they were quickly out of my sight.

I continued trotting after them and caught up at the lad's house as my colleague took hold of his collar.

As I approached huffing and puffing, the boy's father emerged from the house and shouted, "Whoa, be careful with him, he's got chronic asthma."

I thought at the time, 'Christ, if I can't catch a 15 year old boy suffering with chronic asthma, there's definitely something wrong.'

That was my wakeup call and from then on, I chucked the cigarettes, drank less alcohol and took up running, cycling and hiking. It was the best wakeup call of my life!

To have an advantage over the average criminal, all Police Officers should follow five disciplines in their lives;

Don't smoke,

Don't drink alcohol to excess,

Don't take illegal substances,

Keep your body weight down,

Exercise three times a week for a period of at least twenty five minutes each session.

I can guarantee that a Police Officer following these five rules will be fitter overall than the vast majority of the people they deal with and feel better for it.

Unless of course like me, they chase after a youth on foot, slide on a frosted footpath, crash into a wooden stile and go arse over tit into a blackberry bush which then takes fifteen minutes to untangle yourself from, and end up with two severely bruised shins, numerous small cuts and scratches all over the body and a week on sick leave!

(The pain was nothing compared to the piss-take I got from my colleagues for losing a prisoner).

The Stolen Vehicle Squad used an old yellow coloured unmarked Vauxhall Cavalier to patrol around the car parks in the city in an effort to catch thieves in action. I had my thinking cap on one day and thought about the fact that when a marked Police car patrols around the city, everybody watches it to see what it's doing or where it's going. However, no one gives a second glance to the hundreds of taxis that pass by.

I managed to obtain a taxi roof sign which we fitted with magnetic strips around the base so it would adhere to the roof of the Cavalier, and we painted the letters WAAC and PRIVATE HIRE on the front and back. Only my partner and I knew the initials stood for WE ARREST ALL CRIMINALS.

We had the taxi top sign for about three weeks during which we caught two burglars and a few car thieves as a result.

However, one of our colleagues decided to drive the car at seventy miles per hour on the motorway. The taxi top sign flew off and went straight under the wheels of a very large lorry following behind. That was the end of that.

After about four years in the Shoplifting Squad, I took on the newly created role of Local Intelligence Officer for Newcastle City centre, and worked with a female civilian who I will call Notsobright for reasons explained later. Notsobright had been in the job as long as I, and had seen all the tricks and heard all the jokes. She still enjoyed a good laugh and I've actually seen her run out of the room in fear of peeing her knickers with laughing so hard.

Prior to becoming my assistant, she worked in the front office at Pilgrim Street where she dealt with members of the public. The lads always played tricks on her and she was usually wary of suspicious telephone calls.

A new Chief Inspector took up position at Pilgrim Street and rang through to the front office. She answered the phone and he said, "Hi, it's the new Chief Inspector, could you do me a favour?" Notsobright did not recognize the voice and said suspiciously, "That's not the Chief Inspector, who is it?"

The boss assured her he was who he said he was, but she would not accept it. Convinced she was the victim of a practical joke, she said, "If that's the Chief Inspector, I'll sit on your face," and put the phone down on him.

Minutes later, the Chief Inspector walked into the front office with a brown paper bag over his head, with a hole cut out the front and his tongue waggling through the hole.

For a number of years after the fitness bug hit me, I took part in the Northumbria Police Cheviot 2000 fell race, which was a twenty-three mile event over the wildest parts and highest hills of the County. The event was held in June, with a meeting on the Friday, the race on a Saturday and a piss up award ceremony on the Saturday night, and then everyone returned home on the Sunday morning. Notsobright used to go with her kids to marshal the event, and we all stayed in a caravan.

However, one year the owners sold their caravan but offered a relatives van on the same site.

The caravan site was split in two, with the main road running between, and a site office on each half where keys could be collected. Notsobright told me the new caravan was on the other side of the road. I presumed she meant the other side of the main road and attended the appropriate office. I asked the receptionist for the keys to the numbered caravan, which she handed over.

The caravan was clean but I was surprised to find personal belongings such as underwear in the drawers and food in the cupboards.

We stayed for the weekend and left the van absolutely spotless on the Sunday morning. Notsobright left a note saying how nice our stay had been and could we book it for the same time next year.

About a week later, the Manager of the site rang us to say we had stayed in the wrong caravan and the absolutely furious owners were suing the site owners.

Notsobright was one of the four or five marshals manning a point known as Uswayford each year on the Cheviot 2000 race. The location was high up in the Cheviot Hills surrounded by wild moor land and forests. It was a beautiful place if the weather was nice but bloody awful when it was raining.

The marshal's got water from the nearby stream, chlorinated it, and if the weather was good, would get a barbecue going for their selves.

Sometimes, when I worked with Notsobright, it became evident that she wasn't the brightest button on the jacket, sometimes she didn't think things through, and one year at the Cheviot 2000 event, she proved my estimation completely correct.

I remember it was a beautiful hot sunny day. Not ideal for racing over moors but excellent for the marshals who had to stay at their points for hours.

It started when she was asked to take a water container down to the stream and fill it up. She put the neck of the container on the bed of the stream so as it filled up, it sucked in pebbles, creatures and sandy grit off the bottom.

Of course, no one realized until the racers had carried on past Uswayford and started drinking the stuff later on!

Next, she was asked to chlorinate the water but instead of putting a few tablets in each container, she put them all into one. Again, no one realized until we started drinking water that tasted like a bloody swimming pool!

Lastly, towards the end of the event, after all the racers had passed the Uswayford point, she was asked to dispose of the barbecue, which she then tipped out onto the moor setting fire to the dry grass and heather!

Yep, definitely not the brightest button on the jacket.

Country Boy, who you will remember I worked with in uniform, used to marshal some of the Cheviot 2000 races and one year he was asked to man the point on top of Hedgehope Hill, the second highest hill in Northumberland.

It was forecast to be a brilliant day and he suggested to his wife that they should both go for the day and have a picnic.

He told his wife to pack a rucksack with drinks and food which she then loaded into the car, and off they set.

On arrival at Langleeford valley just below Hedgehope Hill, Country Boy got the rucksack and heaved it onto his back thinking, 'she's loaded this up well, it's heavier than I thought.'

They set off climbing the 474 metre steep gradient and half way up, Country Boy was bent over double with the weight on his back. The neck of his shirt was soaked with the sweat pouring down over his face.

As they reached the top, he was bent over so far his nose was nearly touching the ground. He dropped the pack off his shoulders causing it to thud and sink slightly in the soft peaty turf, and he said, "What the hell….," as he opened the pack and saw she had packed tins of pop, tins of salmon, tins of fruit, tins of hotdogs, etc.

Country Boy and I used to go hiking together in the Cheviot Hills and on one occasion, as we were climbing up the Cheviot, the wind was blowing a gale and it was freezing cold with rain stinging the cheeks of our faces.

There was no conversation between us and we weren't enjoying the experience at all.

Country Boy was behind and slightly below me as we climbed, and unbeknown to him, I had brought with me a joke snot. This was a fluorescent green length of rubber about 15 centimetres long which you dangled from one nostril.

I positioned the false snot hanging from my nose, turned, and as Country Boy looked up at me, he pointed and yelled, "Ahhh, you've got a gilbert," before realizing it was a joke.

I'd never heard that expression before and the two of us burst out laughing until there were tears in our eyes.

We didn't get to the top that day, the weather was atrocious.

CHAPTER 6
BACK TO UNIFORM

A pair of 1950's handcuffs and key. Good for use at work or home.

After three years of Local Intelligence boring work, I ended up back in uniform on the streets of Newcastle City centre.

One night I was on mobile patrol on the Quayside when I saw an old Ford Transit van apparently being driven by a woman with long blonde hair.

As the van went around a roundabout, I noticed the driver had suddenly changed into a man with short cropped dark hair. Intrigued, I followed the vehicle over the Swing Bridge and stopped it on the Gateshead side.

As I spoke to the driver, who remained in the driver's seat, I could see he was very nervous, and I noticed a blonde wig tucked down the side of his seat.

It crossed my mind that this guy could be a robber and was even more suspicious. I could see he was wearing a white shirt but I was unable to see the lower part of his body. When I asked him to step out of the van, he said, "Well, it's a bit embarrassing." I said, "Not for me it's not, get out," totally unaware and unsuspecting of what I was about to see. He opened the door and stepped out wearing a tight black mini skirt, black stockings and very high black stiletto shoes.

A portly Officer worked on the shift in the front office and he was a valuable expert in computers, useless on the streets but excellent as a front office man.

We were on an early shift and had received notification that a Frenchman was believed to be in the Newcastle area and was believed to be in possession of a gun.

The information provided a description of the suspect and warned he may be dangerous.

Later that morning, a man bearing the same description came in to the front enquiry desk and spoke to our portly Officer. The Officer, on hearing his French accent, realized it was the circulated man, and pounced on him, managing to lock him up and retrieve a loaded pistol from his possession.

With the Frenchman safely locked up, the portly Officer returned to the front office and locked the loaded gun in his drawer to be examined and made safe by firearms Officers who had been requested to attend.

As the portly Officer was about to go on his break, he told a Sergeant where the gun was and that firearms Officers were on route to the station, and off he went for a well-earned rest.

Shortly after, the firearms Officers attended, the gun was made safe and secured in the firearms safe.

The Sergeant then acquired a party popper, a small indoor firework that went off with a loud bang, and positioned it in the drawer with a piece of string attached to the inside of the desk and the party popper.

When the portly Officer returned to the front office, the first thing he did was open the drawer to check if the gun was still there, and as he pulled the drawer open, the party popper went off with a bang, the cardboard disc from the popper hit the Officer between the eyes and the paper streamers from the popper went over his head and down the sides of his face.

For a second he sat motionless with his eyes wide, mouth agape and in total shock as everyone around fell about in hysterics.

He later said that he fully believed he had been shot and when he felt the paper streamers on his face, he thought it was blood trickling down!

Before the same portly Officer got a permanent job in the front office, he was out patrolling one day when he received a report that a man had jumped into the river Tyne at the Quayside in an apparent suicide bid.

However, the shock of the cold water must have made him change his mind, and he had swum to the side and was clinging to metal ladders affixed to the quay wall.

The portly Officer attended and on locating the man, he went down the ladders and grabbed the man by the clothing on his shoulder, but couldn't lift him back up.

So, just in case the guy changed his mind again, the portly Officer hung on to him with one hand, while holding onto the ladder with the other, awaiting the arrival of the Marine Division boat from just the other side of the river.

The Marine Division Officers arrived in an inflatable dinghy some minutes later, and loaded the suicidal man into the dinghy.

They then told the portly Officer to climb back up, but having hung on for so long in the cold, his muscles had locked and he was unable to go back up the ladder.

The Marine Division lads positioned their dinghy below him and told him to let go of the ladder and just fall back into the boat.

This he did, but as his overweight body hit the floor of the inflatable dinghy, the suicidal man shot up into the air, fell straight back into the river and had to be rescued a second time.

CCTV had a big impact in Newcastle city centre as crime dropped successfully over a number of years after their installment. It was unbelievable the amount of shagging that was caught on camera, and I fully believe a lot of people were aware they were being watched as they carried out their sexual encounters.

One night, our shift cameraman observed a male drunk stagger through Princess Square. As he watched, he saw a pair of legs in the top right hand corner of the screen. He moved the camera to see a girl sitting on the backrest of a street bench with her feet on the seat and her legs wide open. A male was kneeling in front performing oral sex on her. The drunk walked straight past them without giving them a glance. However, the cameraman was no longer interested in the drunk and, having notified a nearby patrolling Officer by radio, he continued to watch the couple.

After a minute or so, it became obvious that the male was not feeling too good as he collapsed onto his back on the ground. The female got down off the bench and squatted over him. She obviously knew first aid and that she should loosen tight clothing. She proceeded to loosen the male's trouser belt!

She then realized there was a more important matter to attend to. She stood up, walked a few metres away, squatted down and pissed.

She then returned to the still comatose male, straddled over him and wiped her parts on his shirt.

Just then, the uniformed Officer arrived as the male started to come to. The male worked himself with the Officer and was arrested for being drunk and disorderly. The female later attended the front office at the Police Station and enquired how long her boyfriend would be detained, as she had to go to school in the morning. She was only sixteen years of age!

Newcastle City centre had its fair share of public houses and nightclubs, the doors of which were manned by 'bouncers' or door supervisors as they prefer to be called.

Nearly all of the nightclubs had a policy of searching customers before they entered the premises and we used to get a fair number of calls that the door supervisors had found illegal drugs on someone.

I received such a call one night and arrested a guy who had hidden small bags of powder in his shoes, obviously with the intention of selling the packages in the club.

Because he was a drug dealer I decided to attend his home to search it with a drugs trained dog to find any other drugs he may have had.

He lived alone in the Gateshead area and when we attended, it was obvious that the house was an absolute drug den.

The dog handler took his Springer Spaniel in but said it was a waste of time because there was powder all over the place which impregnated the carpets. The curtains, wallpaper and other soft furnishings were saturated with cannabis smoke.

When we came out of the house, I watched as the drugs trained dog cocked its leg to take a piss and then promptly fell over onto its side. It got up and walked over the drive head butting the garage door. Again it fell over with its four feet sticking up in the air.

I said to the dog handler, "What's wrong with your dog?" He replied, "Oh, he's probably high on the drugs, he'll be alright in the morning!"

Being probably the oldest Officer on the shift by this time in age and service I was respected by younger members and probationers. However, the respect was not returned as I took great delight in playing tricks on these same colleagues.

One of the probationers had been in the Army and had done everything, according to him. Everything he said revolved around his military career.

I concocted a bogus message to our Inspector one night shift, informing him that a pigeon cull was to take place in Newcastle City centre over two nights, and a Police presence was required to ensure there was no interference from animal rights protestors, and to ensure that only the maximum number of 200 pigeons per night was killed.

The Inspector, who was aware that it was a wind up, passed the message to Army Boy, instructing him to meet the City Council Vermin Control

Officers at Greys Monument in the very centre of the city at midnight. Army Boy was full of it, telling everyone how he had been picked specially due to his knowledge of firearms.

At midnight, most of the shift went to the CCTV room and watched Army Boy on camera as he stood waiting at the monument.

At half past midnight, the Inspector radioed Army Boy and told him the people he was to meet had been delayed at Tynemouth where they had been culling seagulls.

He asked Army Boy, while he was waiting, to spot any likely targets and count the pigeons in the immediate area to see if there was enough to kill. We then watched as Army Boy strained his neck skyward, pointing up to the roofs with his finger and counting to himself. He still hadn't grasped that it was a setup, and eventually we had to save him by calling him back to the station.

Whenever Army Boy realized he had fallen for one, which he invariably did, he always had this little smirk on his face and knowing look as though he wanted to say, 'I knew it was a setup all along.'

In this job you are never too old in service or age to learn a lesson or two, and sometimes the tricks you played on probationers didn't always go as planned.

A young girl joined the shift and one night we had a report of intruders in a derelict warehouse near the Quayside.

We attended and found a door open leading into a large empty storage room which had stone pillars throughout. There was no power to illuminate the building and we had to use our torches to conduct a search.

I stayed downstairs while the other Officers, including the young female probationer, went through a doorway and upstairs to continue the search.

When it became evident that there was no one in the building, I heard the Officers coming back down the stairs. From the voices, I thought the probationer was coming down first, so I hid behind a pillar at the bottom of the stairs.

As the first Officer emerged through the doorway, I jumped out and as I did so, the leading male Officer automatically swung his baton that he had in his hand, missing my head by a centimetre.

I definitely got a bigger fright than he and learned my lesson not to frighten adrenalin pumped up colleagues.

Sometimes the tricks you played were better than you intended due to unexpected factors.

Another female probationer on the shift made the mistake of telling me she was frightened of ghosts when we were on night shift. Remember what I said earlier in this book with the rat story.

Well, I told her a ghost story and frightened the life out of her.

Pilgrim Street Police Station consisted of two buildings separated by the Magistrates Court. The building on the corner of Pilgrim Street and Market Street was the main Police Station open 24/7, and the building in Market Street was used for administration and refreshments, and was locked to the public.

Later that night, we returned to the station on Market Street for a break and she asked where the female toilets were. I sent her along a corridor where painter and decorators had been working, towards the male toilets.

As she returned, I was waiting behind a cupboard wearing the decorators dust sheet over the top half of my body. As she came along the corridor, I jumped out in front of her causing her to scream and run off.

I later apologized and directed her to the female toilets on the upper floor.

However, I forgot and never thought to mention that telephonists worked 24/7 on the same floor.

As the probationer walked down the dark corridor, she glanced through an open door, and saw the body of a female lying on the floor in the dark room.

The probationer gave a terrifying scream and ran back downstairs. I nearly choked on my sandwich as she ran into the room and grabbed me in a quivering hug.

It turned out that one of the telephonists had a troublesome back, and the only relief she got was to lie down on a hard surface for a few minutes.

You may have formed the impression that I constantly played tricks on people, in particular probationers. That may be true to a certain extent but quite often, I was the victim of tricks too.

A number of times I was given a note asking me to contact a Mr. C. Gull or Mr. C Lion on a particular telephone number only to find I was ringing the local Coast Guard or Edinburgh Zoo. Another favourite at the time was a message for you to contact Sam Arriton. On telephoning, you get the local Samaritans group, a charitable organization that offers counselling to distressed people!

There was a particular area of the City centre frequented by men looking for other men for sexual encounters. We had a number of complaints on Sundays in particular, when families would use this area as a shortcut from the Quayside and witness some indecent activities.

So it was decided by the shift Inspector to carry out plain clothed observations in the area over a few Sundays to discourage the activities.

One weekend, he told me I was to carry out the task and asked if I could dress 'appropriately.'

We were working a late shift that Sunday and, for a joke, I wore a pair of black Lycra cycling shorts with a sock stuffed down the front, and a capped sleeve tee shirt with the words 'WHIP ME BIG BOY' emblazoned across the front.

At the start of the shift, everyone coming on duty met in the parade room to receive their duties, details of events over the past twenty four hours, items of local intelligence, etc.

I waited until everyone was on parade, and as I walked down the corridor past the Inspectors Office, I heard the early shift Inspector say, "What the fuck...," followed by roars of laughter.

I walked into the parade room and everyone burst out laughing, except my Inspector who put his hands to his face and shook his head.

I raised my hands and said quizzically, "What?" then turned to reveal that I had cut a large hole out of the back of the shorts exposing my bare buttocks. That's when everyone fell off their chairs in hysterics.

It took at least an hour or two for the shift to get back to normal, and no, I didn't wear the attire to do observations!

The same Inspector wanted to see the area we were observing for himself and volunteered to join us one Sunday afternoon. We tried to discourage him but he insisted he wanted to see what went on in the area.

Dressed in civilian clothing, he joined us and stated he would have a walk around by himself. Again, we tried to advise against this but he insisted.

The Inspector walked into the area and sat on a bench next to a man. As he did so, the guy suddenly looked at him and without any warning, grabbed the Inspectors testicles while making lecherous noises with his lips.

The Inspector jumped up horrified, arrested the guy and never went back to the area again.

I was parked up with a colleague one night in a plain Police car looking for car thieves on the Quayside. We were wearing plain clothes and were parked facing a tunnel which runs under the Swing Bridge. We had been there a few hours and our conversation had dried up so things were getting a bit boring. But then we saw a couple approach our car from the other side of the tunnel.

The girl was wearing the shortest of miniskirts and had bare legs. Before emerging from the tunnel on our side, they stopped a few yards in front of the car, and the guy pushed the girl up against the tunnel wall.

In their drunken erotic state they either didn't realize we were there or simply didn't care.

They started kissing passionately and his hand was groping her breasts before dropping to her crotch. He then put his hand up her mini dress and pulled down her black thong to her ankles. While he wrestled with his trouser belt, she kicked off the black thong.

A group of people walked past and I heard one of them making a comment about a hairy arse, at which lover boy turned on them in an aggressive manner.

We immediately got out of the car in anticipation of trouble, approached the couple flashing our warrant cards, and told them to find somewhere more discreet. The female ran off leaving her black thong on the ground.

Later that night, we returned to the station and as I entered the Bridewell, I saw the same male and female under arrest for being drunk and disorderly.

The female was being searched and I said, "Mind, she's got no knickers on."

The female looked at me and said, "Eeee, how do you know?"

I said, "Because I've got x-ray vision," at which she turned to the searching Officer and said, "Eeee, has he really."

Thick tart.

I was with a female probationer one day when we received a report that an elderly man had collapsed and died of natural causes in the City, and the body had been conveyed to the local hospital where we were to attend to take a report.

The probationer was not too keen and explained to me that she had never seen a dead body before. Unfortunately for her, I am a great believer that probationers should deal with every subject they possibly can because sometime in their career, they'll most likely come across the same kind of incident. Also, in the Police service you can't pick and choose jobs just because you don't like dealing with a particular type, you just get on with it no matter what.

We attended the hospital mortuary but the probationer was worried sick and very nervous. I tried to console her but the mortuary attendant wasn't helping matters by joking on, pointing to bodies saying things like, "That's Mr. Kellogg's, he's a cereal killer."

I showed her how to examine the body but she kept her distance and looked away most of the time.

After we completed the report, she ran out of the hospital with tears streaming down her face and immediately lit a cigarette to calm her nerves.

Later in the day after she had composed herself and recovered from the ordeal, I jokingly told her that she was required to attend the post mortem the following morning.She was devastated and unknown to me; she later told a female Sergeant who took great interest saying, "I've never been to one, I'll ring the mortuary and see if I can go with you."

The following day, they both attended the mortuary to watch the post mortem being performed.

When I was told where they were I was horrified and thought, 'The poor probationer, she'll kill me when she finds out I was only joking!'

However, when they returned to the station, they both were in a state of happy excitement and explained that they found the experience very interesting. The probationer had no problems at all, probably because she was accompanied by another female and someone she could trust.

So what started as a joke, turned out to be an educational experience for the probationer and the Sergeant. I was so pleased about that result!

A female civilian worked in the front office at Pilgrim Street Police Station on our shift, and her teenage daughter had a habit of burning her early morning breakfast at home on a regular basis.The house was usually stinking of burnt toast when the civilian returned home later in the day.

She only lived about three miles from the station and one morning; she received a telephone call from her daughter saying, "Mam, the house is on fire!"

The civilian told her to ring the fire brigade and to get out of the house. She then arranged for someone to take her home.

An Officer picked her up in a marked car and as they pulled into her street, there was three fire tenders with flashing lights and firemen running back and forward to the house, with smoke pouring from the back and front doors.

The Police Officer was looking left and right as he drove up the street, and then said to the civilian, "Which house is yours then?"

Even murders have their occasional funny moments as was proved in a particular incident in the City centre.

I was the first Officer at the scene of a domestic incident after a divorced husband and wife, both alcoholics with a long history of violent confrontations, had been arguing and the ex-wife had suddenly lashed out with a kitchen knife and stabbed the ex-husband straight into his heart.

When I got there, a male passer-by had been summoned by the female to assist, and he in turn flagged me down.

I entered the ground floor two bedroom flat to find the body on the floor propped up against a settee. He was obviously dead and the ex-wife and the passer-by were arrested on suspicion of murder.

Having assisted the ambulance crew in an attempt to revive the deceased for about thirty minutes, we were instructed to leave the house to preserve it for forensic examination.

C. I. D., Scientific Aids, (the forensic lot), and the Pathologist arrived and did the necessary, the Pathologist examining the body, the Detective Inspector sketching a plan of each room, and Scientific Aids videoing the scene.

When everything was completed, the body was removed to the morgue and two Police Officers were left to guard the rear door and open front door.

After about fifteen minutes of everyone leaving, The Police Officer at the front door heard a noise behind him from inside the house and as he turned, he saw a little bald man walk along the passageway towards him scratching his head and asking, "What's going on," much to the shock of the Police Officer.

The Police Officer said, "Where have you come from," and the man replied pointing back inside the house, "Out of there, I've been asleep."
The Officer then said to him, "Well, you're arrested on suspicion of murder," to which the little bald man screamed, "What!"
It turned out that the same fellow had been in a drunken sleep under the blankets in one of the bedrooms and everyone had missed him!

I was doubled up with another probationer one afternoon in a high speed marked car, when we were required to park up along a road from an observation point, where Officers had been watching a group of men who they thought were stealing a caravan.
The caravan had been hitched up to a car, and the suspects had adjourned to the local pub, apparently for a bit of Dutch courage. We were to wait until they got back into the car and start to drive off before pursuing and stopping them.
The probationer and I waited for a few hours, and then he asked if we could nip back to the Police Station so he could relieve himself.
I no sooner drove towards the station when the shout went up over the radio, they were moving.
The probationer moaned that he was a little desperate but we had no choice, we went after the car and caravan.
We followed it into a cul de sac where I stopped it and spoke to the driver. It became immediately apparent that the caravan was his, but I could smell alcohol on his breath and asked for a breath sample. He agreed and I went through the procedure, asking how long it had been since his last drink.
He said it had only been a minute ago and as he said it, the probationer gave a little louder moan knowing that in order to comply with the law, we had to wait another nineteen minutes before we could test him.
By the time I completed the test, the probationer was doing a little street dance, tightly clutching his crotch and grinding his teeth together.
The test proved negative and the driver was allowed to continue on his way. We then returned to the station as fast as we could.
Before the car stopped, the probationer had the door open and he leapt out.
He raced up to the front door of the station only to find it locked. He stood trying to open it with his legs twisted together and crotch still clamped in his hand, and then raced in to the gent's toilets knocking over buckets and brushes with such a clatter, that people looked out of their offices along the corridor towards the commotion.

Other Officers and I were in stitches as we entered the toilets and heard him moaning and sighing in ecstasy as he pissed for what seemed a full four minutes.

When you double up with someone from your shift, they were your partners. Someone to rely on if trouble brewed,someone to express your worries to andsomeone to look to for advice.

However, even though you may think whatever is said between you and your partner is strictly confidential, you must always remember that nothing in the Police service is confidential. That word just doesn't exist. There are things you should never ever discuss with your partner, especially if they are of the opposite gender.

I was with a young Policewoman patrolling about in a marked car when I noticed that she could not sit still in her seat. She was squirming around trying to find a comfortable position until eventually I had to ask what was wrong. She told me that she was suffering from a bad case of vaginal thrush, (for medical students who may be reading this - also known as Candida). Someone had told her that yoghurt was a good remedy for this fungal ailment and so, in an effort to stop the terrible itching, she had smeared her lower regions inside and out with yogurt.

Unfortunately, what her medically unqualified advisor hadn't mentioned was that you should use natural unflavoured yogurt.

The dozy thing had used strawberry flavoured yogurt and it took her a week to fish the seeds out. (I'm sorry, that was the most inappropriate term to use.)

Chapter 7
Whickham. Bit of Quiet? Not Really.

A 1950's battery torch. It fitted perfectly in the pocket, but not in the hand.

In July 1999, I decided I needed a change from the city and moved to Whickham which was about six miles south west of the City, and which was a nice mixture of small country community villages and towns.

I had reached the top of the hill of my career and was starting to head down the other side towards retirement.

Seven years to go and I thought it would be quieter than the City centre. I was wrong. If anything, it was a lot busier and I ended up working my bollocks off for the remaining years.

Political correctness had set in with a vengeance and a person had to be very careful of what they said, or what they input on the Force computer.

However, sometimes opportunities arose that a person such as me could not ignore.

The shift I was on consisted of members who were young in age, young in service, or both.

We were working a 5pm - 3am shift one night and at about 1.30am eight of us were sitting parked up in a personnel van outside a local nightclub. Everyone was tired and silent and watched as a male and female came out of the club.

The male was wearing a white shirt and the female wore a very short mini skirt.

As we watched, the male bent down slightly as the female jumped up on his back with her legs wide open wrapped around his waist.

"Fucking hell, it'll take his mother ages to get that stain out of his shirt," I remarked.

There was a deathly silence from my fellow shift members and I thought, 'Oh no, complaints, investigations, sacked, etc.'

However, the following day a young lad off my shift said to me, "I nearly pissed myself laughing on my way home last night thinking about what you said in the van."

I said, "Well why didn't you laugh at the time," and he replied, "Well nobody else did and I thought I would get into trouble just for laughing."

It was a terrible shame for me because I enjoyed a good laugh and was used to that type of quick response humour.

Another time we were parading on prior to going out on patrol and the Sergeant was reading out incidents that had occurred over the past twenty-four hours.

He said that someone living in the Dunston area had a dead chicken put through their letterbox.

I said, "What, someone has put their cock through the letterbox?"

The Sergeant said, "No, a dead chicken."

I said, "Aye, that's what I said."

That got a few laughs.

At the back end of December 1999 I was asked to return to Newcastle City centre to assist on a murder enquiry involving the gay community.

I had been a Lesbian, Gay, Bisexual and Transgender Liaison Officer for about eight years and had a few contacts within the community.

Each day we were given tasks such as interviewing possible witnesses, making enquiries with various businesses, speaking to other organisations, etc.

On one occasion, I visited a man at his home who was openly gay and who frequented the area where the murder had occurred.

The man lived alone and on entering the premises, I noticed how dirty and disheveled the place was.

I spoke to him in his sitting room and asked if he knew the murder victim. He said, "Oh yes, I knew him, in actual fact that's his cock there," and pointed to a line of silhouette type drawings of erect penises on the wall, similar to the drawings of airplanes that World War Two pilots put on the side of their aircraft to indicate how many they had shot down.

As I looked, he said with pride, "That's all the men I've shagged," and then added, " shall I put your cock on there?"

That's when I realized that this guy was absolutely bonkers and I made my excuses and ran!

I returned to Whickham in April 2000 and I was asked to act up in the rank of Sergeant quite frequently.

I was the only supervision on a late shift when we received a report that a guy had not seen his female neighbour, who lived alone, for four days.

Two Officers and I attended the house and we noticed the curtains were open and a light was on in the upstairs bedroom.

We banged on the doors and shouted through the letterbox but received no reply.

I was concerned for the occupant and decided that we had to smash the backdoor lower pane to check the house, and then proceeded to hit it with a hammer which we acquired from the neighbour.

The glass smashed with a loud crack and we crawled in. I was first, followed by the other two Officers.

The passage was dark and as I slowly walked down, I glimpsed movement to my left and jumped, which made the first Officer behind me jump, then the second behind him.

I looked and saw it was a full-length mirror on the wall and the movement was my reflection.

Letting out a breath of relief I carried on, then saw the reflections of eyes ahead of me and instantaneously realized they belonged to a very large Rottweiler dog sitting at the bottom of the stairs. I jumped which made the first Officer behind me jump, then the Officer behind him.

I then saw that it was a full size stuffed toy dog.

Letting out another breath of relief we proceeded up the stairs and as I got to the top, one of the Officers behind me pointed to the half open bedroom door and whispered, "I think she's in there."

I said, "What the hell are you whispering for, we've banged, shouted, smashed the door with a hammer and jumped out of our skins twice!"

Unfortunately, he was right.

A local hard man in the North East was shot and murdered, and a number of books were written about his life.

I actually met him twice some years prior when I worked at Newcastle City centre and I found him to be a canny guy, although he had a lot of heavy criminal friends and had spent time in prison for his violence.

A colleague and I worked Chopwell area one night and had a report that a well-known fifteen year old male from a neighbouring village had threatened a couple and their son.

Locals had already informed us that this particular individual was causing a lot of trouble.

We attended and after taking the threats report and offered advice to the victims, we left the area, but as we do so we received a further call from the same couple stating their window had just been smashed.

On returning to the village, my colleague and I saw the individual in question standing at a bus stop not too far from the attacked house.

There was no evidence that he was responsible but we stopped, and as we spoke to him, it was obvious to us he was as high as a kite on something. We got the usual bragging verbal diarrhoea as he said no one could touch him as he had too many contacts, and he had wads of cash, more than we would see in a lifetime.

I had never encountered this individual before and got sick of his attitude in the first minute. I put my face close to his and said, "You know (the hard man who was murdered a few years ago)."

He said, "Aye," and I said, "Well the same thing's going to happen to you. One dark night someone will come up to you, put a gun to your head and POP, you'll be dead." In a deep slow voice, my colleague said to me, "That was his dad!"

You may recall that near the beginning of this book I mentioned that sometimes Police Officers can be a little too eager for their own good. I was working with an excitable colleague one day who had my nerves shattered and my body exhausted in a matter of a few hours.

It started when he spotted a car in the middle of a field. As we drove past, he suddenly jumped up and down in his seat shouting, "Turn back, turn back, there's a stolen car in that field!" By the time I turned around, the car had disappeared.

We then spent thirty minutes searching surrounding fields and woods only to be later informed that the car belonged to the farmer who was dropping off bales of hay.

Ten minutes after finalizing that non incident, as we were driving past a car park, my colleague again jumped up and down in his seat shouting, "Stop the car, stop the car, there's a man in that car park covered in blood."

As I jammed the brakes on he leapt out of the car and ran over into the car park. I followed him as he approached a car and pulled open the driver's door, only to expose a man eating a pizza with tomato sauce all over his face!

I couldn't work with him on a permanent basis; I would have had a heart attack. After all, I wasn't in my prime anymore and needed to take it easy.

During all of my service, Police Officers wore dress shirts as part of the uniform, with an extended front and back tail. This was probably to stop the shirts from coming out of your trousers. It didn't work. Not when you're involved in a battle rolling around the floor with drunks.

A lad on my shift was seen in the gent's toilets at the station taking his Police shirt off before entering the closet.

He was later asked why he did this and he said, "Once, I went to the toilet leaving my shirt on, but as I sat down, I didn't realize I had sat on my shirt tail, and I shit all over my shirt!"

Explain that one to your mother!

It was 4am and I was taking a few measurements for a road traffic accident that I was dealing with.

I was at a traffic light controlled junction outside a newsagents shop and there wasn't a sole in sight. The radio was quiet and it was an ideal time for such a task.

As I stood in the middle of the road with a clip board in my hands, I heard a door open.

I looked up and saw a totally naked man emerge from a house next door to the shop. I immediately thought he was sleep walking and being aware of the dangers of waking a person in this state, I remained silent and watched.

I also thought to myself, 'It must be colder than I realize.'

The man walked from the house to the newsagent shop door, picked up a bundle of recently delivered newspapers, unlocked the shop door and put the bundle inside.

He then locked up and turned to return to his house, but on seeing me standing in the road in full uniform, he suddenly froze.

For a moment neither of us spoke, and then the man said, "There's normally no one about at this time," as though that was an excuse for his state of undress.

I replied, "Well I'm here, and I didn't want to see that!" pointing to his winky, which had definitely shriveled even more since spotting a Police Officer.

The man put both hands over his small appendage, which was by that time a bit late and disappeared back into his house.

I wonder if he told his wife.

A security guard worked at a certain establishment on my patch and one night he reported that his metal hut had been broken into.

I attended and straight away I was unhappy with the truthfulness of his account.

He told me he had locked the hut and went out on patrol but on returning, he saw the silhouettes of two men running away. On checking the hut he found his brand new very expensive mobile phone, which he had left in the hut to recharge, had been stolen.

There was no sign of a forced entry. The thieves had allegedly unplugged the charger from the phone and left it, and nothing else had been taken.

I took the report but as I drove away and thought about it, I became more convinced that the report was false.

I did a U turn and returned to the hut to find the security guard outside, vomiting on the footpath - a classic sign of guilty nerves.

I told him I was unhappy with his report and I intended to take him home to examine the receipt for his expensive top of the range mobile phone, to prove he actually had one.

He got into the back seat of the Police car and I said to him, "Do you see the junction line at the top of the road there," indicating to the main road junction about five hundred metres away.

He replied, "Yes," and I said, "Well, you've got until we reach that line to tell me the truth about what happened."

I don't really know what he thought was going to happen when the car reached the line but I drove towards it very slowly and all the time I was saying, "We're getting closer, you better tell me, nearly there, it's getting closer."

As I neared the junction line my voice was getting quicker and more urgent until just half a metre from the line, his body suddenly shot upright in his seat and he blurted out with his eyes nearly popping out from their sockets, "Okay, I've been lying, I'll tell the truth!"

I stopped the car as the security guard lay back into his seat with an obvious feeling of relief that the back seat hadn't ejected or something, and he explained he had lost his phone and had mistakenly thought that if he reported it as stolen; he would have been able to claim through his employers insurance.

What he hadn't counted on was a wily old fox being sent to take the report!

The following incident has nothing at all to do with my Police work (other than I was still a serving Police Officer at the time), but ladies and gentlemen, this is my confession to a heinous crime.

This is the true story of entrapment, unintentional torture and murder, to which I put my hands up and regretfully take full responsibility for.

We had a problem with mice at home. The little buggers found a route from my back garden into the kitchen, and every morning, we found tiny black torpedoes on the kitchen floor.

Being the conservationist that I am, I decided to purchase a humane trap with the idea of releasing the rodents in the nearby woods as far from the house as possible, because you always think they'll make their own way back.

The trap was plastic, shaped like a wedge and pivoted in the centre, so when the animal entered, the trap rocked and a hatch dropped trapping the creature inside.

The first time I caught one; I put the trap in my pocket and headed off with my dog into the woods.

The day was bitterly cold with a white hoar frost covering everything.

Now, there were a couple of very important facts that did not enter my head as I set off. Firstly, trapped rodents release a considerable amount of body fluids for such a small size, and secondly, a human being, or any mammal come to think about it, does not walk with a perfectly smooth action. So whatever is in your pocket tends to bump about quite a lot as you walk.

So, I had a poor little mouse trapped in a plastic container - which incidentally, wasn't leak proof - banging about with every step I took - covered in its own urine and excreta.

I reached a small stone bridge over a frozen lake, and realizing the dampness in my pocket, I took the container out and tipped the unfortunate mouse onto the stone parapet. The mouse plopped out and staggered about in a bewildered drunken like state, and before I could do anything, promptly fell over the edge and onto the ice below.

I was unable to reach it and watched as the mouse laid spread eagled on its back looking up at me with its little beady black eyes, its body heat slowly melting the thin ice beneath it. You can see what's coming can't you.

Slipping through the ice, it slowly descended into the black murky depths staring up at me as it disappeared.

It was just like the scene from the Titanic film where Rose let go of Jacks hand and his body slowly sank out of sight into the darkness.

I can only imagine the very last thoughts of the poor mouse as it stared up at me, the last image it ever saw, 'YOU BASTARD!'

During the last eight years of my service, I was a qualified self defence instructor. I trained Police Officers and Specials (the volunteer civilian section) how to defend themselves and use their equipment such as batons, handcuffs and C. S. sprays.

I trained the Specials once a month and formed a very good relationship with them.

They were all great people and as keen to do the job as anyone but a few of them were 'wannabe's', and showed their dedication to being Police Officers by wearing tee shirts emblazoned with 'F. B. I.' or 'L. A. P. D.'

I suppose they were a bit like the train and bus spotters I mentioned earlier.

They all attended my retirement party and presented me with an engraved glass tankard and a baseball cap and polo shirt both bearing '619 STATE ELEVEN.'

619 was my Police number throughout my service, and state eleven was what you declared yourself as on the radio to the control room at the termination of your shift.

So in effect, 619 was off duty.

I thought this was ingenious and very apt because now, I really was off duty - permanently.

CHAPTER 8
THE END OF AN ENJOYABLE CAREER

Guarding the Royal yacht H. M. Y. Britannia with a stick!

There are so many true comical stories to be told about the Police service such as: the time a policewoman in the Mounted Section was sitting astride her horse at a local football match, when one of the passing supporters said to her, "Hey missus, your horse is sweating a lot."

Turning her head slowly towards him and glaring down, she replied, "So would you be if you'd been between my fucking legs for two hours!"

Or, when two Summons and Warrants Officers travelled by car to Edinburgh to bring back a prisoner who had been arrested for failing to appear at Newcastle Magistrates Court.

On the way back with him, they stopped at a roadside cafe to get some refreshments.

One of the Officers went into the café while the other remained in the car with the prisoner.

As they were waiting, the Officer turned to the lad in the back seat and said, "While we're here lad, do you want to have a run off?" (A polite way of asking, 'do you want a piss?')

The prisoner held up his hands and said, "No, no, I'll go back and face the music."

I could have made up stories, such as about the male and female Officers who were teamed up together in a van one night shift. The control room was unable to contact them by radio and a search of the area was conducted. The shift Inspector located the van parked up down a quiet country lane, and on approaching the vehicle, the Inspector could see it rocking on its springs and could hear activity in the rear.

On peering through the rear windows, the Inspector saw the Officers naked, and the Policewoman was whipping the Policeman across his back with the detachable roof aerial. Bloodied red wheals were evident on his flesh.

The Officers were taken back to their station, and when the Policeman was later examined by a Police Surgeon, the doctor put in his report, 'it was the worst case of van-aerial disease I have ever seen!'

Yes, it's funny but not half as funny as something that has happened in real life with real people involvement.

Every Police Officer could write a book about their experiences whether they be funny, sad, horrific, unbelievable or whatever.
I tend to dismiss the unfortunate things that happened in my service and would rather remember all the good times, and there were many of them.

The job changed so much in my thirty years.
We became computerised, armoured, C. S. armed and politically correct.

The latter change had a devastating effect on the humour of the job which became sterile because everyone became frightened of discriminating against others or upsetting someone.
There were threats of being sued or of internal disciplinary charges being brought and I personally think, as I indicated at the beginning, because of the lack of humour, people's health will be affected due to stress.

Hopefully, the good humour will return, because without that humour, the job becomes abysmal!

The job did me alright and I loved every minute of it. As I said I can look back at even the bad times and remember there was a hell of a lot more good times.

I had the time of my life over the thirty years and can say with a hand on my heart, I would do it all again if I could be 19 years of age and go back to 1976!

Gordon Shepherd

Lightning Source UK Ltd.
Milton Keynes UK
30 January 2011
166590UK00002B/57/P